I0104794

The Bridges of Madison Railroad

By John Brough

narratuscreative | **narratus**press

THE BRIDGES OF MADISON RAILROAD

©2018 Charlie Wise | Madison Railroad. All rights reserved.

No part of this book may be reproduced or transmitted in any form, or by any means, electronic or mechanical, included photocopying, recording or by any information storage or retrieval system, without express written permission from the author or Madison Railroad.

ISBN: 978-0-9990752-3-4

Published by:
The Madison Railroad

In partnership with:
narratuscreative | **narratus**press
P.O. Box 1413
Hamilton, OH 45012

Design: **narratus**creative | **narratus**creative.com

Produced in the United States of America

PREFACE

The Madison Railroad, as it presently exists, contains one of the largest concentrations of ancient stone arch bridges in the United States and the largest cluster in the state of Indiana. Between North Madison and North Vernon, 23 miles, there are to be found 10 significant arches plus multiple small stone crossings of tiny streams and ditches. In addition are five major stream crossings, all currently equipped with steel bridges. The two newest have concrete decks. Each of these structures feel the weight of 21st century train traffic to this day. Between Madison and North Madison, on the famous Madison Incline, one and three quarter miles presently inactive, we find three more stone arches and culverts of varying size to include the granddaddy of them all—that is the Crooked Creek Stone Arch, at the foot of the hill. Were it to talk, oh, the tales it could tell.

Work on the Madison, Indianapolis & Lafayette Railroad (MI&L RR) began 182 years ago at North Madison. The first portion built is that noted above. It is all extant to this day. The first train operated 180 years ago out of North Madison. Forty years ago, in 1978, the Madison Railroad came into being and keeps on railroading successfully, now going into its fifth decade.

STEEL WHEELS KEEP ON TURNING

The manner in which this ancient line and these ancient structures are cherished and lovingly cared for is remarkable. The line has been re-purposed, very successfully modernized, while always keeping in mind the historical significance of the property. At the same time, every dollar expended is spent wisely and with careful attention to value. The entire operation of the Madison Railroad is first rate and commendable.

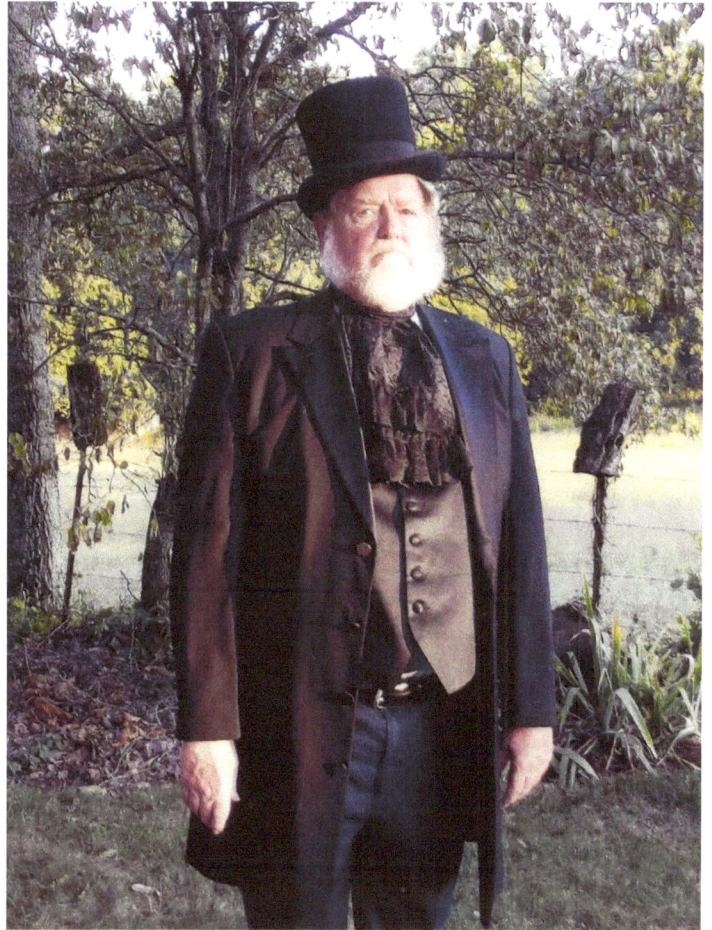

Fall 2016, John Brough, aka Charlie Wise, at home in East Tennessee a few days prior to his departure to North Madison, IN to mark the 200th anniversary of the groundbreaking for the first railroad in Indiana. The Madison, Indianapolis and Lafayette Railroad.
Photo by Dian Wise

My special thanks go to the management team at the Madison Railroad: Cathy Hale, Roger Fuehring and Casey Goode. They have been most helpful in providing necessary, historically significant company records, proofreading, guide services in the field and the answers to multiple questions, in addition to hospitality and friendship. Any and all mistakes and errors or omissions are solely the responsibility of the writer.

PART 1

A Short History of the Madison, Indianapolis and
Lafayette Railroad Company and Successors

THE PIONEER DAYS

The current Madison Railroad is the southern portion—and the oldest portion—of the first railroad built in the state of Indiana. An initial question is: *Why plan a railroad from the Ohio River to the State Capital of Indianapolis and on to another major river, the Wabash, at Lafayette?* The answer: to connect the landlocked state capital with two navigable waterways, the Ohio at the south end and the Wabash along with Wabash and Erie Canal at the north end. The line between Indianapolis and Lafayette was constructed by others so is not a part of this study. A railroad was ultimately constructed from Madison, a thriving port city of 8,000 industrious people, to Indianapolis. In the time of President Andrew Jackson, Indianapolis was called "The Village at the End of the Road" and was much smaller than Madison.

The "village" had no navigable river and no good roads. Pikes of the day featured seasonal snow, ice, mud or rutted and rough dust, providing no reasonable avenues of travel and commerce. The entire interior of the state suffered a similar isolation and developed more slowly than riverbank and lake shore communities. The rest of Indiana was however not the capital city, Indianapolis was. Thus it presented a more acute problem. A canal was explored and found not feasible. Seeking a solution, the legislature on February 3, 1832, only 16-years after statehood, chartered what became the Madison, Indianapolis and Lafayette Railroad (MI&L). At the time this was an act of faith in the unknown. After a few years the line from Madison to Vernon (and on to Indianapolis by 1847) was subsequently built, becoming the first railroad in the state and the fourth west of the Appalachians. By extension, the bridges and stone arch culverts etc., from Madison to North Vernon were the first built in Indiana. A true pioneer railroad.

It was originally desired that private capital would build the railroad. However, private money was not available for a leap of faith of this magnitude. It was, at the time, very speculative and expensive. By 1835 a wave of Internal Improvement fever swept over the states of the Old Northwest—Indiana coming down with a serious case of it. The folks in charge thought they had plenty of money and they almost did, for a while. Accordingly, it was decided the state treasury would fund nine canals and the MI&L Railroad. Of the 10 projects, only the railroad survived to include all of it except the portion from North Vernon to Columbus, which was abandoned in the 1970s.

The MI&L, as previously noted, was a pioneer. Some mistakes were made and some overbuilding took place. Railroading in Jacksonian America was still in its infancy, very experimental in nature. Definite standards for what worked and what did not, what was necessary and what was not had not yet been developed. Much of early railroad building was by trial and error with a fall back by the engineers to canal standards. Canals had been around much longer. The Erie Canal, 1825, in New York spurred much development in all states with Great Lakes shoreline. When canal builders encountered heavy grades too steep for locks, they built inclines, also called inclined planes.

The first survey was ordered in March of 1836 to determine the best route from Madison to Vernon. The largest challenge for the locating engineer was the one and a half mile portion from Madison on the river to North Madison, greater than any challenge faced in the rest of the 29-mile survey, combined. They harked back to what worked well for a canal and opted for an inclined plane or the "Incline" as it is commonly referred to. The shortest distance between two points is a straight line but in hill country, not necessarily a good choice. Reducing grade requires a circuitous routing, adding miles of track to be built. The Madison Incline is a nearly perfect tangent to this very day.

The railroad was formally authorized by the legislature on June 20, 1836 for 1.3 million dollars. Construction contracts were let in September. The first ground was broken at North Madison on September 16, 1836. Construction was to be in both directions from this point. Seeing the difficulty in building from North Madison to the Madison riverfront, the initial plan was to first build northwest toward Vernon, just to get something up and running. The topography was much less challenging. That area did however include five major river crossings and many smaller streams—no major grades though. The first rail was put down in

May, 1838. Indiana had an actual railroad, albeit tiny and incomplete. The future looked bright indeed.

A case can be made that the portion of the MI&L constructed with state funds was overbuilt. As noted earlier, railroad building was an inexact science before 1840. Early engineers did not really know how strongly to build so if they could afford to do so, they erred on the side of safety. Safety translated into overbuilt. The stone arch bridges are a classic example of this. The trains of the early day featured locomotives weighing a dozen tons or so. The stones still hold firmly today, essentially as built, where built, by the pioneers. They now support weights ten times those of the Jackson presidency.

Rail is another example. The MI&L was one of the first lines west of the Appalachian chain to use imported T-rail. It weighed 45 lbs to the yard, was rolled in England and cost $75 per ton delivered to the Madison riverfront. Though much lighter than rail of the present, it was essentially a smaller copy of the 115- 156 lbs rail used worldwide today. An alternative to T was domestic strap rail. Hugely cheaper and lighter, 19 lbs to the yard, it was widely used before 1850. By 1860, nearly all strap rail nationwide had been replaced because it did not work well at all. Other pioneer lines learned this the hard way, but not the early state-built Madison. The apparent overbuilding saved them much trouble. However, the portion of the line built with private capital north from Griffiths, aka "Queensville," 28 miles from Madison toward Columbus and beyond, did use strap rail. They soon regretted their false, if forced, economy. With extremely limited funds, the entrepreneurs really had no choice. However, the maxim, "you get what you pay for" applied then as well as now.

Postcard circa 1910 looking up hill showing huge cut in the foreground and the State Hospital bridge in the background. **Charlie Wise Collection**

With a seemingly huge supply of funds buoyed by a national business boom, the die was cast. The powers that be ordered the contractors to build the Madison to top shelf standards. No skimping, especially on rail and bridging. Thus, for the arches more expensive stone was used in place of much cheaper timber. This decision was aided by an abundance of stonemasons and good stone nearby. Ditto, plenty of good timber and good carpenters. However, stone is far better account, stronger, fire resistant, flood resistant and it lasts indefinitely. The first arches of the Madison have proven this every day for 180 years and counting. Untreated timber, while cheap, had a life expectancy of five to 10 years. It is combustible, can go wobbly in very high water and is subject to collapse under tonnage. Stone arches, by their design, become stronger as more weight is applied from above. Overbuilding the Madison arches turned out to be a very good idea.

In 1839 the railroad formalized an already accomplished fact in the form of an early standard to be followed under the Internal Improvement Act:

"Streams of a larger class requiring greater waterway—and yet not so large as to require a timber bridge will be crossed by means of arched culverts formed of substantial stone masonry and varying in their span from 6 to 30-feet." The directive went on to add detailed specifications for arch construction.

Five major streams are crossed between North Madison and North Vernon. Due to length of spans needed to get from one side to the other and the height above the waterline, stone arches were not used here. They could have been though as some long, tall and multi arched bridges, still serving today, were in place "back east" at this time. Instead, bridges were opted for. No good iron or steel of the size needed was available in Indiana so builders resorted to timber. The five bridges in question cross Middlefork, Big Creek, Graham Creek, (aka Graham Fork, Muscatatuck River), Otter Creek (aka South Fork, Muscatatuck River) and Muscatatuck River (aka North Fork). The combined length of these five is just short of one-fifth mile. The abutments on both banks and the support piers in the stream crossings were constructed of stone and well made indeed. Some of the fine masonry is still visible as it survives to serve the Madison Railroad today. Much more old stone is not visible but still serving as it is, encased in concrete applied by many successive rebuilders over the many decades. The original 1838-1839 timber is long gone of course, succumbing to decay, fire, water and war. An attribute to timber bridges, in addition to being economical, is the ease of quickly rebuilding them. Local carpenters had plenty of work until iron and steel became readily available.

Steel ultimately did come to the Madison well after *The War Between the State*s. It is unclear exactly how many rebuildings the five bridges underwent. Two things are clear: The first, not one of them ever failed under a train; the second, the present day Madison Railroad has continued the major rebuildings into the 21st century. This keeps the bridges all well maintained, up-to-date and modern. The aesthetic appearances of the retired antique super structures are gone, to be sure, but the railroad is a better and safer operation for it. All the while, below all this rebuilding and replacing lies the original Jacksonian era stonework found in the piers and abutments. These are rock solid after 18 decades and counting.

The primary focus of early construction of the railroad was North Madison toward North Vernon, though much work was simultaneously being done grading and excavating the huge cuts and fills of the Incline. The plan was to get something up and running so the taxpayers could see tangible results of the expense. Secondarily, a completed line of any significant length could begin to generate passenger and freight revenue. The builders were forced to do it the hard way. All imported supplies and material to build toward the north came primarily via the Ohio River and were wagon freighted up the hill from Madison to North Madison. This on horrid roads. Such was the condition of Southern Indiana in 1838. The status quo virtually screamed for improvement.

The first imported rail was put down in North Madison near the State Highway 7, crossing near the brow of the hill in May 1838. Rail laying followed surveyors, grubbers, graders, stonemasons, timber cutters and bridge carpenters moving north. By late fall, about 15 miles of line was completed to Graham Creek, (aka Graham Fork, Muscatatuck River). Here was a major river crossing, at the time named Graham Ford. A good place to halt. Seventeen miles, including a two mile carriage ride up the hill from Madison, seemed a decent distance for an initial run. The time was ripe as well. It was just before winter set in to restrict much further progress until Spring 1839.

Under those first 15 miles of 1838 iron was a good solid roadbed and 20 water crossings of various sizes. Structures included two major stone arches, both 65-feet long, Harberts Creek in Wirt and Camp Creek in Dupont. These two, both still serving essentially as built, are the oldest major stone arch railroad bridges in the state of Indiana. In the first 15 miles are 6 other significant stream crossing arches and multiple stone culverts, many still serving in 2018. This is a true testament to the genius of the arch concept, the ability of the early stone masons and the durability of Indiana Limestone.

Also within these first 15 miles are two major river crossings, Middlefork, 180-feet and Big Creek, 192-feet. (Note: measurements are spans as of today.) Variations may have occurred during several rebuildings involving different bridge designs and materials since 1838. Timber, iron and steel superstructures come and go but good stone, well built, is permanent. Much of the mason's art, both covered in concrete or visible, dates to the original construction.

The first passenger trip took place on November 29, 1838. Like much else in the lives of the pioneer, things did not exactly go as planned. The MI&L definitely intended to showcase their brand new locomotive from Baldwin Locomotive Works, Philadelphia. She would have likely been christened the "INDIANAPOLIS" upon successful delivery to the railroad in Madison. Sadly, aboard the ship en route from Philadelphia to New Orleans, the vessel was nearly overcome by storm. The locomotive was cast overboard to save the ship and her crew. Pioneers are nothing if not resourceful. Kentucky to the rescue. Madison borrowed the "ELKHORN" from the Lexington and Ohio Railroads. This locomotive was transported by water from Louisville to Madison. It was then towed up the hill on a rutted mud road by struggling teams of draft beasts aided by block and tackle. Once again doing things the hard way. By late November, all was made ready for the "ELKHORN" to do the honors out of North Madison.

The initial trip was a success. The governor and many dignitaries climbed aboard the primitive cars. Likely, many had never seen a locomotive, much less ridden behind one at a rollicking good speed of 8 mph. In 1838, this was fast, very fast, a huge leap forward. All passengers seemed pleased or kept mum on any displeasure. Upon return to North Madison the dignitaries were all transported by carriage down the hill into Madison to a mighty fine supper. Her task completed, the ELKHORN was sent home. The MI&L bedded down for a winter of relative quiet and rest after the milestones of history laid in 1838.

As the MI&L was being graded in 1837 and rail was being put down in 1838, the funding euphoria of 1836 began to give way to a deep financial panic (recession/depression) that affected the entire country. Slowly the money supply ran low but the state

1837 Wirt Arch over Harbert's Creek on the Madison Railroad, looking east, 2016. This is the first arch north of North Madison and therefore the oldest major structure and the first to feel the weight of a train in the state of Indiana.
Madison Railroad Collection

pressed on. In late 1838, the end of track was Graham Fork for the first train. As construction progressed, the line to Vernon, likely just short of the South Fork, Muscatatuck River (aka Otter Creek) was opened for service on June 6, 1839. This included the longest bridge (later installed by the Pennsylvania Railroad), Graham Creek, (280-feet present length) which was originally 166' when line first opened. Soon, the bridges over the South Fork, Muscatatuck River, 144-feet and the North Fork, Muscatatuck River, 189-feet were placed in service. Also included was the first grade crossing separation west of the Allegheny Mountains, the Pike Street Arch and the adjoining retaining wall in Vernon. Several smaller arches were built by 1839 as well.

Two MI&L locomotives arrived safely in Madison in early 1839. They were named the "INDIANAPOLIS" and the "MADISON". Money was still tight but Hoosier optimism ruled the day. The pioneers progressed ever north toward "The Village at the End of the Road".

As construction moved north from Vernon, Queensville (aka Griffiths) located 27.8 miles from Madison, was reached by the steam cars on June 1, 1841. "Steam cars" was an early definition for any train propelled by a steam locomotive. It normally referred to passenger or mixed trains. The state, totally exhausted financially, ran out of money to press on. Internal Improvements that looked so rosy in 1836 now appeared as infernal improvements, which had bankrupted the treasury. There was no more money anywhere to borrow and no collateral anyway. When Indiana adopted a new Constitution in 1850, not borrowing money by the state was included. That restriction still exists today, brought on in part by Madison, Indianapolis and Lafayette Railroad.

The focus herein is the portion of the line financed and built by the state of Indiana, specifically the portion still in existence and operated/owned by the Madison Railroad. After many financial maneuvers and as many said, "shenanigans, larceny and chicanery," the state took a huge loss but did finally get rid of the railroad to private builders/operators. By then, business conditions had significantly improved. Construction resumed. Standards were much less stringent north of Queensville than south. Strap rail, etc., was the norm but the project was completed. The 86 miles from Madison to Indianapolis was open for business on October 1, 1847. "The Village at the End of the Road" finally had an all-weather transportation artery to the outside world.

On September 16, 1836, as work started north from North Madison, it also began south of that point down the hill toward the riverfront wharves in Madison. The incline included crossing Crooked Creek passing through three major cuts and over multiple expansive fills. "Stupendous" described it in the construction days and still describes it now. This piece of work is a tangent plane ascending 413-feet from the river to the hilltop plateau at a grade reaching 5.89%. The Madison Incline is the steepest non cog mainline railroad grade in the country. It is presently inactive as rail and track/roadbed conditions are poor. It certainly does make for nice a hike though. More time, effort and money were spent building and opening the Madison Incline for service than on the remainder of the state-built railroad between North Madison and Queensville.

Three major cuts in the hillside were required. The first, nearest the foot of the incline, was 100-feet deep. The second called the "Big Cut" was 117-feet deep and 1,150-feet long. Eighty to 100 Irish laborers worked on digging this one alone, being paid little in the way of money but supplemented with plenty of whiskey. The third, nearest North Madison, was a 40-feet deep excavation. The rock in all three cuts was blasted loose by gunpowder and then carted off by either man or beast. Much of the spoil from the diggings went to build the massive fills, including both sides of the granddaddy of them all, the Crooked Creek Stone Arch Bridge. Stupendous indeed.

The name or names of the skilled bridge builders and master stonemasons who built what is now called the Madison Arch are lost to history. Their edifice was finished in 1841. The stone arch and the adjoining fills suffered severe damage and partial destruction during the September 1846 flood of near biblical proportions. A wooden trestle was erected over the void. This patch required two-weeks to build at a cost of $2,060. The Crooked Creek Arch was repaired/rebuilt circa 1862 exactly as it was originally built by the pioneers. It stands today as a testament to those ancient craftsmen.

On November 6, 1841 The Madison Incline was opened for traffic. A locomotive of unknown name and one freight car came down the hill from North Madison and proceeded to the wharves of Madison. There, boarding and clinging to any spot available, between 75 and 100 locals rode the first train up the hill to North Madison. That momentous trip took a reported 11 minutes. Apparently locomotives on the incline were not found to be particularly desirable after the initial run. For several years thereafter the practice of a team of eight horses powering one car up the hill was employed. For many years, even after the advent of cog and later, adhesion locomotives, down-bound cars were propelled by gravity, controlled by hand brakes.

As noted earlier, Indiana was bankrupt by 1841. Railroad funds were totally depleted by the time the line reached Queensville, 29 miles from riverfront Madison. It was left to others to finish the line and then operate it. The pioneers, financed from the public coffers, built well indeed. But, the Madison Incline, famous yet today, was not such a good idea as the passage of decades has shown. It certainly seemed to be a good idea at the time though.

PART 2

Prosperity

THE GLORY YEARS—1847-1853

The MI&L pioneer days ended at Queensville in 1841. Subsequently, several financial maneuvers took place over the next six years. The taxpayers were essentially looted courtesy of the Internal Improvement fever of 1836 and the following financial panic of 1837. Ultimately, absorbing the monetary loss and bowing to the lessons learned, the state of Indiana got itself out of the railroad building enterprise. Then, Indiana got itself out of the railroad owning business as well, albeit with a fleecing at the treasury. During this time of upheaval, uncertainty and shenanigans, the line went through several name changes. The most commonly used was the Madison and Indianapolis Railroad, or M&I, which perfectly described the core mission. We will primarily use M&I henceforth for simplification.

In October 1847, the M&I reached Indianapolis. This was done with new owners and new operators. All the pioneers had departed the scene. The line possessed a monopoly. The M&I was the only viable means of reasonably-priced and prompt transportation. The M&I opened the capital city to the outside world. Indianapolis grew, the counties, towns and villages served by the M&I grew, while Madison, in the sweet spot as the port city, boomed. The M&I connected it all and was instrumental in converting "The Village at the End of the Road" into the railroad hub of Indiana and a major player in the Eastern USA rail grid. As to Madison, evidence of that mid-19th century small town booming wealth is easily found still today. It is everywhere, including the M&I Incline and the Crooked Creek Arch.

For quite a time, the line enjoyed more business than it could handle. The track from Queensville to Indianapolis, built by private money, was not nearly as well built as the original portion financed by the taxpayers. Instead of long lasting and rock solid, the 1841-1847 contractors subscribed to the theory of build quick, build cheap, get it running and upgrade it later. They were not alone. Many of the pre-1900 railroad builders followed this theory. Across the land, most were soon upgraded. However, some of the quick and cheap remained in that condition until abandoned and a small portion, lightly used, remains this day. Due to the influx of trade, the M&I began their upgrading immediately. Immediately was not soon enough for the line's harshest critics. Service was slow and often unreliable due to severe congestion.

The M&I management team brought on line new locomotives as fast as they could pay for them, often with borrowed money. In 1839, the line possessed two named steam engines. By 1847, it owned 11 and by 1853, 22 locomotives plied the rails supported by the bridges of the Madison. This is an average of one locomotive for approximately every 3.8 miles of main track for the 87 miles between Indianapolis and Madison. With every new locomotive purchased, improvements came with them. Technology and the inventive genius of the American craftsmen were on the march. An 1853 model was barely kin to those of 1839. Even at that, all needed much maintenance often and all were very labor intensive. Keeping them on the road pulling trains took a lot of effort and provided employment for many. The M&I shops were in North Madison, at the top of the hill, east side, between the tracks and current Hwy 7.

The shop complex hummed with activity. In addition to maintaining all the locomotives, passenger cars and freight cars, the mechanical forces even home built some freight cars from the wheels up. It seemed as though there would never be enough. In addition to caring for the rolling stock (cars and engines), the track structure received much attention, especially north of Queensville. The strap rail was removed and replaced as rapidly as possible. It was not a moment too soon. Strap rail was a nightmare with the ends curling up under trains, called snake heads, and just generally shattering under tonnage. It was gone from the main track by 1853. Untreated timber exposed to mother earth in the southern Indiana climate had a life expectancy of 5 to 10 years. Thousands of cross ties were replaced every year. Bridge timbers lasted longer but even above the water and soil, they deteriorated over time. The stone arches and culverts needed precious little attention.

March 2017, Mile Post 27 Arch at MP 27 over a small stream, looking west. . **Charlie Wise Collection**

Yet, the congestion persisted and the criticism, especially in the press, pummeled the owners and operators of the M&I like hail stones. Not enough cars and too many hogs! Handling live stock to the river was a big portion of the M&I business. Indiana farmers produced more and more every year once there was an efficient manner by which to get them to market. So, place a newspaper editor or an aspiring local politician on a passenger train made up of less than ideal equipment which is then delayed by a broken down hog train in the way. Try to imagine the flurry of non-complimentary prose that flowed. Simply stated, too much of a good thing can become a bad thing. Better too much than too little. As opposed to the M&I, many early lines did not have a good traffic base at all and so they stagnated. Some withered and died early on.

One of the most prominent men behind the completed M& I was James F. D. Lanier of Madison. Born in 1800 in North Carolina, he came to Madison with the family in 1817. He involved himself in state government as well as banking. He became the president of the Bank of Indiana and concentrated special efforts at the Madison branch—his hometown. He was involved with the construction of the M&I and positioned himself well to become a major stockholder by the time of its completion in October, 1847. He had earlier assisted the state of Indiana financially in extricating itself from the canal and railroad business, deriving significant income from it all. Thus he definitely enjoyed the prosperity of the M&I monopoly of the 1840's and 1850's.

Mr. Lanier built his Madison mansion in 1844. It stands proudly today. Widowed in 1846, he re-married in 1848. His expanding banking interests, with an emphasis on railroad stock trading and financing, took him to New York City in 1851. He partnered with Richard Winslow to open the banking house called Winslow and Lanier. He never again lived in Madison, but did not forget the community. He continued to be active in the affairs of the M&I as a major stockholder and behind the scenes financier.

If Mr. Lanier was behind the curtains as the dignified, genteel, financial manipulator, John Brough was center stage as the gruff and crusty M&I persona commonly in the public eye. He was born in Marietta, OH, orphaned at age 11. He began his professional life as a journalist with several newspapers in Southeastern Ohio. He clerked the Ohio Senate, served as state representative and state auditor. When the Whigs swept the Ohio Democrats from power in 1844, he looked west and decamped to Indiana. He was elected president of the Madison and Indianapolis Railroad in 1848. His tenure closely paralleled the glory years.

Brough oversaw much of the rebuilding and refurbishing of the line as described above. Lanier raised the money and Brough spent it all plus any other funds he could get access to. Most but not all was spent wisely. There was, after all, the major flaw in his resume—the matter of Brough's Folly—to be described a bit later. Yet, in spite of his good efforts, the journalistic hailstorm, criticism, congestion and complaining editorials, continued. This large and corpulent man had a thick skin and simply sloughed off the criticism and pressed on. He had a monopoly on his hands, a cash-cow in modern jargon, and was clever enough to understand that this is the sort of things a monopoly brings about. He sometimes seemed to thrive on the controversy.

On balance, John Brough, always flamboyant, was quite good for the M&I. In addition to modernization of the portions of the line last built and already outdated, he attempted to get ahead of the levels of business flowing to the line. In today's parlance, he thought outside the box. An example is his early embrace of the telegraph, completed over the entire length of the line in 1853. Railroaders could now communicate with each other to make operations more efficient. Businesspersons and others from Indianapolis to Madison could coordinate arrangements to assist in their daily decisions concerning shipping schedules, ordering supplies, etc. In view of the fact that the intercity telegraph was invented only nine years earlier and first used as an aid to railroad operations in 1851 on the Erie RR "back east", this 1853 installation in Southern Indiana is quite remarkable.

The ugliest blemish by far on the legacy of John Brough in Southern Indiana is "Brough's Folly" still widely remembered today as much of it is visible in Clifty Falls State Park. Early on, the Madison Incline, "the hill", was found to be the major flaw of the original 1836 Internal Improvement M&I plan. This was due to the severe nearly 6%, grade. After opening day, many locating engineers and surveyors spent numerous hours combing the hills around Madison searching for a better way up from the river. The huge flood of 1848, which took out the massive Crooked Creek Arch, made it even more imperative to find a better way, if one existed. The timber patch in place of solid stone was never thought to be a permanent fix.

The powers-that-be settled on a bypass line which was much longer in distance and designed to accomplish a huge reduction in the severity of the grade. Nothing is ever easy when it comes to building rail lines from Madison up the hill, as Brough and his associates found out. Much of the grading was to be done in rock, in very tough country, requiring two tunnels to hold the grade to an acceptable level. As history played out, these two became the first railroad tunnels built in the state and the first to be abandoned as neither ever saw a revenue train. After several years of trying and $300,000 essentially wasted, in 1855 the bypass enterprise was abandoned. Right or wrong, Brough was tagged as the man responsible for the debacle and so we have what is called "Brough's Folly" to still enjoy in Clifty Falls state park. The 1836 Madison Incline concept remains, to this very day, the best option of all horrid options available to the M&I Railroad builders. After the folly project failed and was abandoned, the Crooked Creek Arch was rebuilt as it was originally constructed. Solid Indiana limestone towering over Crooked Creek in Madison is another, although unintended, tribute to John Brough.

It was mentioned earlier that Brough was quite clever and turned out to be clever enough to get out of Madison while the getting was good. He left Madison before the folly was abandoned and about the time the M&I monopoly on traffic to the Ohio River from Central Indiana was broken. He decamped north to the state capital, to become involved with the Indianapolis Union Railroad and the building of the first Union Station in the USA. He also was president of the Bee Line Railroad. During the War Between the States, he returned to Ohio to be elected governor, prompting President Abraham Lincoln to exclaim by telegraph to Governor elect Brough:

"Glory to God in the Highest. Ohio has saved the Nation".

John Brough died while in office in 1865. Two quotes from his time in politics seem to very accurately describe John Brough. Ohio Historian Walter Havinghurst stated that Brough,

"... is a big bull of a man with driving energy."

Richard Abbott opined that Brough,

"...had a reputation for rough and ready politics with a temperament to match (he was) a blunt, outspoken man who loved to chew tobacco (and thus) presented quite a contrast to his two handsome and dignified predecessors."

The winds of change continued to blow but now, against the prosperity of the Madison and Indianapolis Railroad, rather than in its favor. The monopoly was broken. Several additional lines began to provide service between Indianapolis and the Ohio River, striking it at Jeffersonville directly and via connecting lines, at Lawrenceburg and Cincinnati. Indianapolis became a major railroad hub opening lines of travel and transport in all directions and to most major centers of commerce and population. Waterborne travel began to evaporate and the volume of goods transferred from rail to steamboat diminished. Canal traffic of all types quietly disappeared and before long the canals were gone as well. Of the 1836 Internal Improvements, only the Madison and Indianapolis Railroad survived and more or less prospered. Lanier was in New York. Brough was in Indianapolis. A slow decline was at hand.

PART 3

The Long, Slow Decline

The Long, Slow Decline

Holding on to a monopoly is difficult and doing so without the support of the state of Indiana using its influence via regulations, restricting competing charters, etc., made it nearly impossible. This is the situation the M&I encountered in the early 1850's. High profits and rising traffic levels, coupled with a booming economy, drew competing lines to southern Indiana. By 1853, the M&I had to deal with three competitive routes from Indianapolis to the Ohio River. Plus, Indianapolis had all rail access to the east and to the north and soon, the west. By 1870, 11 rail lines radiated as spokes from the center of the city. "The Village at the End of the Road" had become the rail hub of Indiana. Closer to home, three new spokes extended to Jeffersonville (across the river from Louisville), Lawrenceburg and the prize of them all, the Queen City of the West, Cincinnati. Madison proved to be, in one way or another, inferior to these other river ports as a major terminus for a Hoosier rail line.

Jeffersonville was superior due to proximity to Louisville, a large and growing city by this time, providing access to interior Kentucky and the south. The two were across the river from each other, then a short ferry ride away. Cincinnati was superior due to its size, an established status as a rail hub and being a huge river port. Lawrenceburg was marginally superior due to not having to deal with the Madison Hill, which had become an operating nightmare and a bottleneck of the first order. Neither Cincinnati nor Jeffersonville faced a 5.89% grade getting their trains up from the riverfront either. While there was much more commerce flowing than 10 years earlier, the M&I percentage of the whole dropped greatly as the other lines picked up all the business they could handle. In the freewheeling days before any federal regulation, fierce rail competition was unrestrained, sometimes brutal and constant.

The decline in the fortunes of the M&I was neither sharp nor consistent. Instead it was slow and genteel, with respites. *The War Between the States* found it performing admirably as a busy link between the industrialized North and the battlefronts of the South. During the summer of 1863, General Morgan and his raiders found all the lines of Southern Indiana. He inflicted varying amounts of damage to each. The lines to Jeffersonville and Cincinnati suffered more, but the M&I was not spared. A railroad name change occurred, one of many, but for now we will continue to call it the M&I. By war's end, the line was tired, weary and in need of significant repair and refurbishment—except for all but one of the original stone arch bridges, stone abutments and piers supporting the five large river crossings, that is. The exception was the Crooked Creek Arch in Madison taken out by flood in 1846. Aside from that, all masonry survived in as built condition. The war and fire had no effect on stone.

A cash infusion took place on May 1, 1866, also effecting a significant name change. The Jeffersonville Railroad merged itself with the M&I to become the Jeffersonville, Madison and Indianapolis Railroad. This was a logical combination. Both lines shared the track between Columbus and the city formerly referred to as "The Village at the End of the Road." The Jeffersonville franchise was the better of the two because it reached Louisville via ferry service. Across the river from Madison was rural Kentucky hill country and of course the Jeffersonville did not suffer the Madison Incline. On the other hand, Madison was on the river and significantly closer to the capital than Jeffersonville. The M&I of course had much better arches and bridges, at least south of North Vernon. In the merger, the Jeffersonville was definitely the superior force. The new folks on the scene were definitely in charge. The die was cast. The M&I south of Columbus would decline over time to branch line status. The question then became: *how long would it take?*

The Madison Incline, the M&I's Achilles' heel, proved to be a real problem. Gravity propelled passenger and freight cars went down efficiently enough but the up trip against the 5.89% grade was tough. Horses pulled mightily for about a decade. Then came cog steam engines. This involved a rack device secured to the ties in the middle of the track, designed to engage gear teeth rotating below the engine. While better than horses, cogs were not as good as simple adhesion used on nearly all other railroad track. The cog engines were named the M.G. BRIGHT and the JOHN BROUGH. They served faithfully for about two decades but the cog system broke down often and was expensive to maintain. There had to be a better way to run this railroad.

With the Jeffersonville Railroad merger, came its master mechanic, Reuben Wells. The now JM&I Railroad had a mechanically skilled and gifted man. Wells pondered a solution to the problem of the hill. His answer was a huge, heavy steam engine, no cogs, with ten driving wheels for maximum adhesion. He tested it on the Madison Incline in 1868 and found it to be quite adequate to task at hand. It immediately went to work after the railroad named it in his honor. The REUBEN WELLS shoved cars up the incline at a decent speed and with power enough to handle all the business offered. The several stone arch culverts between Madison and North Madison including the massive present day Crooked Creek Arch, felt the pounding trod of the REUBEN WELLS several times each day. After the first effective adhesion engine proved itself reliable, the cumbersome cog system was quickly removed. The REUBEN WELLS, wood fired, served for almost four decades and is now permanently displayed at the Children's Museum of Indianapolis. A fitting location for a priceless relic of another day and time.

After 1870, the line between Columbus and Madison lapsed into a relative quiet, though the slow decline continued. The line was still well maintained. Ties were renewed and heavier rail was laid on much of the branch. Wooden superstructures on the five long bridges gave way slowly to steel. The only originals that remained from the construction days and the early boom years were the stoneworks of the arches and bridges, plus the grade and alignment. Several passenger trains continued to ply the line. Freight business was decent enough, especially along the riverfront in Madison. After several mergers and such, the JM&I became part of the Pennsylvania Railroad(PRR), lines west of Pittsburgh. Ownership by the Standard Railroad of The World did not stave off the decline. Being a stub end branch was a problem and having the Madison Incline made it more problematic. Operations became a rather genteel nod to the past rather than a look to the future. The PRR did have the deep pockets to keep the line in very good condition.

The Great Depression of the 1930s proved to be a huge financial issue even for the mighty P. Company (PRR). They could not afford genteel any longer as traffic levels and revenue plummeted system wide. On June 30, 1931, the last steam passenger train called at the Madison riverfront.

October 10, 1938, saw the last passenger service of any sort to Madison withdrawn. This run was a month and a few days short of the 100th anniversary of the first passenger train from North Madison to Graham. Passenger service, one train, returned 178 years after the inaugural run. The reconstituted Madison Railroad operated an Indiana Bicentennial train from Dupont to North Madison on September 16, 2016. This marked to the day the 180th anniversary of the original groundbreaking for the oldest railroad in Indiana at North Madison. (Photo on page 22.)

Madison, IN circa 1931. PRR locomotive soon to leave the 1895 passenger depot and shove the train up the incline to North Madison near the very end of steam powered passenger trains in Madison. Depot building is now the Jefferson County Historical Society.
Photo courtesy of the Jefferson County Historical Society

The Madison Incline continued to dominate the thinking on how the branch should be operated. A major problem was the engines, including the REUBEN WELLS. Later, several models of PRR steam locomotives were specially equipped for service on the incline and assigned to the Madison Branch. The REUBEN WELLS was retired. As traffic levels withered, the "hill" power was often used through from Madison to Columbus, with no change at North Madison. On November 18, 1953, the last steam engine was removed from the branch to be replaced by specially equipped diesel- electric locomotives. The switch from steam to diesel between 1950-1960 was complete nationwide, except for a few isolated pockets. Only specifically designed steam or diesel was used on the Madison Incline. This effectively barred a huge preponderance of the PRR vast locomotive fleet from Madison riverfront.

North Madison, IN on September 16th, 2016. At approximately 7:00PM, Madison Railroad locomotive 3, Little Lady, had just powered the Indiana Bicentennial ceremonial torch from Dupont, Indiana. Madison Railroad business car, Legacy, brings up the rear and carried the torch, the torch bearers and dignitaries. **Madison Railroad Collection**

The decline of the Madison Branch coincided with the switch from steam to diesel power in the 1950's. By 1960, old style branch line railroading was no longer profitable. The historic first railroad of Indiana was becoming a shadow of its former self. The owner, the mighty far flung PRR, fell from financial grace due to over-regulation, changing economics and the demise of the passenger train due to competition from autos and airliners. Even The Standard Railroad of the World was not immune to this sea change and in many ways was more susceptible to decay than other lines serving other markets. In an effort to remain financially viable and concentrate scarce money on the lines with the most traffic and the most potential, secondary and branch lines suffered deferred maintenance. Track conditions deteriorated and speeds were reduced, in many cases to 10 MPH. In spite of the shortage of funds, bridge standards were never relaxed. The stonework of the pioneer 1830's on the Madison Branch held solidly as anticipated and cost PRR precious little. However, with traffic levels, service levels and public perception of the P. Company declining, the stage was set for an impending disaster. The possible abandonment of the oldest section of Indiana's first railroad was very real. The mighty had fallen indeed.

PART 4

To the Edge of the Cliff and then Rescue

TO THE EDGE OF THE CLIFF AND THEN RESCUE

The owner of the original Madison and Indianapolis Railroad and its historic stone arches, the once mighty Standard Railroad of The World, the far flung PRR, was truly desperate in the 1960s. So desperate that in 1968, the P. Company(PRR) merged with hated rival New York Central to form Penn Central. It is yet open for debate among historians which of these two companies was the weakest financially premerger. That the marriage was a complete monetary disaster was painfully obvious to all when, in 1970, Penn Central declared bankruptcy. Flat broke. At the time, this was the largest corporate bankruptcy in history. About one half (counting the other bankruptcies) of railroading east of the Mississippi River and north of the Mason Dixon line was, for all intents and purposes, on the verge of extinction. The Madison was a part of the fiasco, albeit a small branch.

Penn Central and other financially embarrassed neighbors were deemed too big and too important to just disappear. Taken as a whole, the bankrupt cluster was needed for the continued prosperity and progress of the nation, but all the parts were not equal as to their value to the country and many were seen to be expendable or even worse, totally worthless or redundant as part of the total enterprise. Thus, many of the lines in existence in 1970 were gone within 10 or 15 years. But the core needed to survive as a viable enterprise was preserved. A variety of political forces were brought to bear in an effort to keep the entire carcass running and serving while a permanent solution could be found.

The federal government put its muscle and money behind the effort to create a lean and profitable northeast/midwest rail system to rescue Penn Central and other lines. In 1971, Amtrak had been created to relieve the private carriers of the financial burden of passenger trains. Also, some outdated regulations, dating from the 1880s, were relaxed. The emaciated company limped along on federal handouts, maintaining the property and rolling stock adequately enough to keep everything on the rails and upright most of the time. Deferred maintenance was the rule of the day—a stop gap measure, as it always is—not a longterm business plan. On April 1, 1976, Conrail was created as a result of a federally mandated and financed complete corporate reorganization.

The folks planning Conrail saw the reality of the situation and understood that much of the trackage owned by Penn Central did not meet the needs of the newly created and hopefully soon to be profitable corporation. Government control was seen as short term strategy, a step on the way back to private ownership. This was farsighted and courageous thinking that ultimately paid big dividends, including corporate dividends. Those came in the future. In April 1976, the lines not absorbed by Conrail were essentially cut adrift, though the ownership of such lines remained with the entity still called Penn Central, no longer an operating railroad company. The Madison Railroad from Columbus to Madison was homeless and thought by many to be as dead as a doornail, much like many other branches of Penn Central which were abandoned and scrapped. This prediction was partly correct. The line from Columbus to north of North Vernon was abandoned and has returned to nature, leaving few traces of its existence.

The strong-willed folks in Madison had other ideas about the original segment of the oldest railroad in the Hoosier state. They likely never gave the stone arch bridges a second thought at this moment of decision, but the strength of limestone over all these years was still there—solid—a constant, silent statement about how things can be done right. Building this oldest portion of the railroad with multiple bridges, arches and culverts was not an easy task and took some time. Bringing the line back from a near-death-experience to vibrant life was not easy or particularly quick either. The local folks put the line on life support and bought themselves some time for the political climate to be ready to save it. Ultimately the muscle of the City of Madison produced a viable pathway for the line from north of the CSX (B&O) connection about a mile or so at North Vernon to the Ohio River to remain open for business. Rail service was preserved in 1978 by a can-do-spirit similar to that of the local folks supporting their community interests in 1836 when original construction began. Good call, Madison.

The road to rescue for the Madison Railroad was not all smooth pavement. Public ownership of a rail line was not particularly common in the late 1970's, though not unheard of. The massive spin off by bankrupt Penn Central (PC) of secondary or redundant lines and branches was a new experience for all. Up until that time rail lines were seen as quite permanent and in no particular danger of quietly disappearing and returning to nature. That all had now changed. In the 20 years following the PC collapse, much of the rail network in the state was abandoned. The surviving large rail lines, the "class ones," spun off much more trackage to independent private operators. They reduced themselves to core operations of high density lines. This strategy succeeded beautifully. The class ones are now stronger than ever. Through it all, some lines, like the Madison, went to public entity operation. Not all of them made it after adoption. The Madison did and it is thriving. Indiana's oldest, with its stone arches and long bridges intact, did survive the tumult. As "Steel Wheels Keep on Turning," the pioneer attitude in Southern Indiana continues to prevail.

In September 1978, The City of Madison Port Authority took possession and began operations on the oldest railroad in the state. Included in this acquisition was a line composed of a standard gauge, single track, non-signaled route from the riverfront in downtown Madison to a point north of North Vernon, approximately 25 miles total. The condition of the property was barely functional and not in good shape by any standard. Decades of neglect and deferred maintenance by the Pennsylvania Railroad and later by Penn Central had taken a toll. Many ties were deteriorated and much of the rail was light in weight by late 20th Century standards. In several locations the rail would disappear below the mud from years of neglect of proper drainage. On the plus side, relatively light traffic density over those same PRR/PC decades had done minimal wear and tear damage to the basic track structure. The line was well located and well engineered in the 1830s. Little changed in this regard by the 1970s with the exception of deferred maintenance.

And how about those bridges? The rock solid arches were and are as good as new. Well maintained by default as they needed very little attention. The five large steel river crossings rested on excellent, though ancient, masonry and were in decent shape overall on start-up day. The original "overbuilding" by the state of Indiana paid off once again. The challenge facing the new operator was significant but not overwhelming, assuming they could hang on for a few decades as the little railroad that could, it did its best just to survive. The Madison Railroad should be, could be and was rehabilitated thanks to those early employees and managers like Larry Keith, that sacrificed long days with few tools and little pay. After a long career in hospital management, Larry still serves on the Madison Railroad Board and is one of the few engineers and the only member of the current day Madison Railroad that is credited with operating the 5.89% incline.

As is often the case, large projects involving public entities and public money are complex. Dealing with the cranky estate of the deceased Penn Central only complicated things further. From 1978 until 1984 there was significant wrangling over funding, purchase of the property, the price of course and obtaining clear titles. Local attorney and former Representative in the Indiana House, Spence Schnaitter, handled the process, facing off against the Philadelphia lawyers of the Penn Central. In the end, The Port Authority of the City of Madison prevailed and from a legal perspective, the line was officially theirs. And what about that small town lawyer from Madison that faced down the Penn Central lawyers? Spence still handles legal issues as Madison Railroad's lead attorney. Because of Spence's help in the State House and his talent in the courtroom, the Madison Railroad was up and running on its own. The current lady in charge, Cathy Hale, was there to witness it all from those modest beginnings.

Between 1984 and mid-2000's, several customers, sensing permanent, high-quality rail service, located along the line. Long, long gone were the ancient industries producing flour, whiskey and processed hogs for shipment over Madison wharves. Southern Indiana was now quite modern in its industries with cutting edge plastics, steel and automotive supply plants leading the way. The vision of the Port Authority was to hold open a viable route for rail commerce to North Madison from North Vernon. Mission accomplished. At the same time, track improvements kicked into gear. The progress was slow, methodical, economical and steady while always forward-looking. It is said that the mythical gristmills of the gods grind slowly but exceedingly fine. This analogy can be applied to the current Madison Railroad.

In 1988, Cathy Hale became Operations Manager. The course was set and has been followed for three decades of progress with flexibility as needed based upon the changing needs of shippers and current opportunities. Between 1992 and 1996, a caboose spotted near the Highway 7 road crossing in North Madison was rehabilitated and became the operating headquarters.

In 1992, the Indiana/Kentucky Electric Company generating plant in Madison received, by rail, several new transformers. These loads are considered high, wide and heavy. Therefore in July 1992, the power company had an engineering firm inspect all bridges, stone arches and culverts. The Dupont Arch failed the

North Madison, IN. The caboose was the office for the Madison Railroad for a few years. Locomotive 3634 is the last locomotive used on the Madison Incline. It is still giving good service weekly. **Photo courtesy of Grover Lowe, former Board Member of the railroad, now deceased.**

inspection and emergency repairs took place over a long, holiday weekend. All others were given a clean bill of health and found to be adequate to the task with no significant attention required. The shipments moved from North Vernon to North Madison and down the hill to the river without incident.

These proved to be the last revenue rail shipments on the Madison Incline from North Madison to the riverfront. Engine 3634, pictured above, and still on the property, did the honors and is considered the last hill climber of the Madison incline. The incline was mothballed by the Madison Railroad. All track from the foot of the hill to the top does remain in place, though some recent erosion makes it a bit unstable to walk along. A few years ago a local preservation trust had enough ties replaced to hold the rails in place. The stone arch bridges and culverts required no attention whatsoever. They are as solid as on day one. The incline is open to foot traffic. It is a really fine place for looking back to the early history. All the massive cuts were made pretty much by man power and animal power, aided by black powder. The huge, high fills were constructed similarly. For those not inclined to hike the incline, a trip to the massive Crooked Creek Stone Arch Bridge just north of Main Street in Madison, will give a good idea of the magnitude, skill in construction and permanence of these ancient works,

The following is reported from an interview with Cathy Hale in April of 2018, as transcribed by W. Roger Fuehring:

The 180-year plus history of the railroad has been marked by many trials, tribulations, tumult and triumph. That is three to one against the survival of the railroad. The actual odds in favor of triumph on the ground were much worse.

In 1996, The City of Madison Port Authority, based on the business model developed by Cathy Hale and encouraged by the then chairman of the board, Jerry Thaden, purchased a significant portion of the huge Jefferson Proving Ground located along the rail line a few miles north of North Madison.

That was the turning point for the Madison Railroad. It was the key moment in history that the line would start to again support itself financially since the early 1850s. The moment that changed everything was based on one very important day in 1996.

The base closure of Jefferson Proving Ground was considered by many as a major opportunity lost by the community. At the time of the closure, Jefferson County was pursuing the Jefferson Proving Ground (JPG) for future development. Madison Railroad was struggling just to keep the bills paid and only survived with generosity from the local communities and rail availability fees paid by the customers and potential customers along the line. The county allowed the Madison Railroad to piggyback on their application for the railroad to purchase the 10,000 square foot engine house (Building 216) and three miles of the original seventeen miles of right way, providing access to Building 216. This would have been a large step for the railroad without adding much new revenue, but Cathy was hoping for the future.

Maybe business will turn around. Hopefully we can support the extra up keep and utilities with such a large building, thought Cathy, along with other worries. The Army, however, rejected the county's application which devastated her. However, Bob Grewe, the Base Closure Coordinator for Jefferson County advised Cathy to submit a letter for a "negotiated sale to a public entity" prior to the joint application with the county. This was to Madison Railroad's benefit, based on the county's failed bid. The other fourteen miles of railroad had already been assessed for scrap value at the request of the Army. Re-purposing the rail had already been ruled out by the Army due to how fragile rail can be if not stacked correctly during shipment. Cathy assumed the fate of the three miles she tried to save with the support of her Board would be removed, scrapped and lost due to bureaucracy along with the other 14 miles of rail. It was a low time in her career and might very well of been the death blow of the railroad.

A short time later Cathy found herself walking into Colonel Weekly's office (the Base Commander) with her head hung low. He immediately snapped her out of her despair from the situation.

"Where have you been? The Pentagon has been trying to get a hold of you," said the Colonel. "They want to see if you're still interested in purchasing the railroad and the building."

Surprised and shocked, Cathy sat down in the Colonel's office, along with Bob Hudson, a civilian working on the base closure for the military. The Colonel made a call and immediately set up a conference call with five other officials, all at different locations. Several of them were on vacation that day and didn't make it on that conference call. As Cathy says, "The military likes to wait, wait, wait and then it is an emergency." On that day, it was providence, as it was with breakneck speed that the callers on the other end gave the impression in the conversation to follow, that a deal needed to be struck.

Someone on the conference call asked, "Are you interested in purchasing the rail and the building?"

Cathy, knowing that they would be lucky if they could gather $10,000 said, "That would depend on the purchase price."

The voice on the phone responded, "That would be based on the appraised value"

Cathy responded, "Well, that would depend on what that appraised value is."

Someone on the other end said, "$85,000."

"What would that include?" Cathy asked.

"The building and the railroad," responded the voice.

"How much railroad?"

"All of it."

"All seventeen miles?" Cathy inquired, knowing that the other fourteen miles was to be scrapped.

"Yes," said the matter of fact voice.

Doing everything to contain her excitement Cathy responded, "I can tell you that we are willing to negotiate for a purchase."

"Can we get that in a fax from you today?" the voice asked.

Yes," responded Cathy. "Can we get a fax from the Army to the effect that we would be purchasing the building, 17 miles of trackage and some miscellaneous items?"

"Yes," said the voice on the other end.

"One last thing. Is the price negotiable?" asked Cathy, as Colonel Weekly's jaw hit his desk.

"No," responded the voice on the other end.

"Well I suppose we can make that work," answered the local high school educated girl to the Pentagon brass.

That same day Cathy returned to the caboose located on Green Road that made up the City of Madison's Port Authority office, and began to pace the floor with nervous excitement. She had less than 45-feet of narrow space in that caboose that she had cherished as the railroad's office since 1992. No more borrowed space in a smoke filled corner of the old Barber Grocery Supply warehouse that was previously used as the railroad's office space. Around 6:30 that evening the fax machine rang out. With less than three rings it picked up and the familiar sound started beeping as Cathy leaned over the discharge tray. The ink roll started printing out a message. At no time since the condemnation suit did the future of the railroad hang in the balance as much as this moment in time. Would the railroad survive another 18 years with upside down revenue? Would Cathy and the employees make it after years of minimum wages or less, including all the unpaid hours put in? Many nights she had been wide awake knowing the need for ties, rail and bridge repairs. The band aids were failing and she knew it. Her optimistic personality was starting to wear thin. Revenue sources were dismal and the future looked dim for the railroad. *Was that future to be or not to be* was the question in her mind as she pulled the message off the fax machine. With all the emotion of the past 18 years she jumped for joy and yelled out: "WE GOT IT!"

That following Monday, the Corp of Engineers wanted to meet with Cathy in their Louisville office. When she arrived she walked into the meeting room full of top brass from the military, attorneys, civilian contractors and others sitting around a large conference table. The room fell silent as Cathy walked in, alone. As she approached the conference table, the room in unison looked behind Cathy towards the door. The moment caught her off guard and then she realized, *they're expecting an entourage to follow.* Without missing a beat, Cathy looked at the group and said, "They decided to send in the big guns." With that the room erupted in laughter as they all took their seats and the negotiations started.

"To Cathy… Who accomplishes more with less than anyone I know. Thanks for your friendship and support."
Terry M. Weekly, Col., USA.

"I guess you know by now that we made a mistake," hinted one official.

"No, what do you mean?" Cathy responded, inquisitively.

"Cathy, we only intended to sell you the three miles of rail that leads up to the engine house," the official said.

"That's not what my fax says," Cathy stated, confused.

"Cathy, we know what your fax says."

Cathy stared down the room full of brass. "Well that's what we were promised," she firmly stated.

"We know that's what we promised and we will honor the agreement, but the price is not negotiable."

Cathy agreed, stating simply, "Well, we will have to just deal with that."

And the future of Madison Railroad was secured.

The Madison Railroad, after a lot of clean up, reconstruction and painting now had a solid brick home base in Building 216 for their administrative offices.

Upon moving into Building 216, the caboose at Route 7 was ultimately removed. Building 216 also provides a very good base of operations for the several employees handling day-to-day operations. In addition to running trains and maintaining track structure, there are cars and locomotives to be cared for. This work is done inside Building 216 which provides a safe, compact and very efficient shop area. Gone and with good riddance are the days of maintaining everything outside in all kinds of Indiana weather. If it is on wheels and needs attention, inside it now comes.

Along with Building 216 came 17 miles of track. As an active military base, the Jefferson Proving Grounds was a consumer

Former Jefferson Proving Ground, near North Madison (Wirt). Looking north with CMPA Building 216 behind Madison Railroad's business car, Legacy. Building 216 provides an indoor shop area for locomotive and car repairs as well as offices and headquarters for all employees of the Madison Railroad. **Charlie Wise Collection**

North Vernon, IN looking north. Locomotive 3634 bringing locomotive 3 onto the Madison Railroad after its long trip from Kennedy Space Center. Vertical tilting target governs movement over the former B&O mainline. Horizontal target allows movement for CSX over the Madison Railroad.
Madison Railroad Collection

of railroad service in great quantities. When the base closed, a significant traffic source was removed from the Madison Branch. The rail connection and the facility remained intact, though essentially mothballed. At present, 14 of the owned 17 miles are used for storage of hundreds of freight cars. This is a lucrative revenue source. Car owners pay for a place to keep excess equipment until needed once again. The Madison Railroad provides the location to do this, plus any switching necessary as well as inspections and transfer from and to North Vernon and the CSX connection.

North Vernon provides access to the entire North American rail network. Car storage provides significant income for The Madison Railroad. This is all attributable to the acquisition of the whole JPG property. In addition, the site may one day be developed for other rail served industries. In summary, the acquisition of the Jefferson Proving Ground property may be the best thing to happen to the railroad since The City of Madison Port Authority gained clear title to Indiana's oldest rail line in 1984.

Progress, like the trains, rolls on. By 1999, the Madison Railroad was financially solvent, requiring no further operating subsidies. This is much easier to say that to do. It came about due to the diligent solicitation of new business, providing excellent service to on line customers and the community, all the while keeping a close eye on cost control. Spending decisions are based upon what is actually needed, not on what is merely wanted. As to current equipment and tools on hand—wear it out, use it up, take good care of it— be it a locomotive, tamper or copy machine, and use it no more than necessary to accomplish the task at hand. In a word, the Madison Railroad is frugal and frugality is paying off. Frugality does not mean being afraid to spend money to make money. Penny-wise and pound foolish have no place in Building 216.

In 2000, Casey Goode came aboard, quickly becoming the Administrative Manager and filling a critical need as the operation continued to grow. If visiting or calling on the Madison Railroad, you will know Casey by her friendly demeanor and professional managing behind the scenes. Additional operating employees have been hired and trained as business increased, creating a very diverse group of engineers, conductors, trackmen, locomotive mechanics and anything else that deals with the daily operation. Ditto with outside contractors and service providers who have come in as needed. The railroad has created a family style operation between all employees, contractors and the communities they run through. All made possible by the step of faith of a financially strapped operation that had the vision of their leader and a supportive Board. Not only was JPG a wise and a significant investment, but the improvements to the railroad have been wisely made based on the anchor of the additional revenues received from JPG. Well Done!

From 2001 through 2008, revenue car loads continued to increase while car storage became a greater revenue source.

Locomotives were acquired when it was wise to do so. The line is well maintained. Track maintenance was and is on a program basis like on most railroads. Programming involves renewing a certain number of ties and a certain amount of rail each year. The program is based upon the average life expectancy of these items and the number of miles of track involved. Oak ties in heavy mainline service have an average service life of five to seven years. This is somewhat extended on lighter density lines. Programming provides predictability and aids greatly in budgeting over several years. Of course, things do happen so contingencies are provided for. Rails may break and ties may be damaged outside the norm. Such matters are attended to immediately.

The first word in the co-joined terms railroad or railway is rail. With no rail, you have no railroad. Steel T rail has a very long service life if properly maintained and sized to the task required. PRR upgraded the rail from south of Elizabethtown at MP 9.5 to the new Jefferson Proving Ground facility at MP 36.7 in 1941. One hundred pounds for every yard of rail replaced older and lighter steel. It serves at present on the Madison and will likely continue to do so well into the future. When Penn Central deeded the property to the Madison Railroad, 85 pound and 70 pound rail laid circa 1900, was still in place between the JPG and North Madison. This was no longer viable in a 286,000 car weight era. The last of it was replaced by 115 lb steel in 2015. A significant main track rail renewal program seems unlikely to be needed in the near term. The last six sticks of 39' small 85 pound rail was replaced just a mile south of Graham Creek in August 2017. The 1941, 100 lb rail could still be found in the adjoining woods all twisted up from a derailment during the PRR or Penn Central days. For the first time in the railroad's history there is no rail on the main line between North Vernon and North Madison that is smaller than 100 pounds (per yard). Another milestone was reached in 2017. The tie condition on the mainline consisted of: 98% of all ties were no older than the year 2000 and over 65% were newer than 2012.

Between 2009 and 2012, The City of Madison Port Authority, under the direction of CEO Cathy Hale, embarked upon a program of bridge rehabilitation. All five major stream crossings were involved. Bridges have a very long life of usefulness. The ages of the bridges on the Madison Railroad are not excessive. In 2017, an 1875 steel bridge on a main line in New York State was replaced at age 142. Bridges are built exceedingly well but not to last forever. Only stone seems to last forever. On the Madison Railroad, the 120-year-old Big Creek Bridge was completely replaced as was the 120-year-old South Fork of the Muscatatuck River Bridge. Bridges over the North Fork of the Muscatatuck River, Graham Creek and Middlefork were modernized as necessary and upgraded to 21st century standards. Little to no upgrading/rebuilding has ever been required for the many 180-year-old stone arches and culverts. While it may be true that nothing is forever, stone installed by expert masons comes pretty close. As the Madison Railroad turns 40-years old in 2018, the entire line is rated for car weights of 286,000 pounds. This is a relatively recent standard upgraded from 263,000 pounds by the North American Railroads. The Madison Railroad may not be as long as the big railroads, but it is just as strong.

In 2014, Roger Fuehring came aboard as Operations Manager and started receiving mentoring by Cathy Hale, CEO. In addition to the Madison Railroad she is involved with paying it forward in assisting other Indiana short lines. This is a common theme with Cathy as so many others, such as Bob Shaw of the Algers Winslow & Western Railway, who did the same for her during those early days of her career. Roger comes as a seasoned hand, with expertise in locomotive maintenance, operations as well as the intricacies of railroad cars and track maintenance. He hails from a railroad family and grew up in a railroad town, Bellevue, OH. He literally learned his craft at the right hand of his father. He was well taught by a master who lived by the motto, "If I think of it, it is possible."

At present, the Madison roster's five locomotives. These are all relatively small compared to main line power but are more than adequate. Some are affectionately referred to in the rail community as "critters." One stands out as definitely not a critter. Engine number 3 was the last locomotive used at the Cape Canaveral/Kennedy Space Center in Florida and is considered one of the favorites for engineers and little kids alike. Number 3, known as "Little Lady", is in a red, white and blue paint scheme with a painting on the cab showing the locomotive orbiting a planet as the name Madison Railroad is spelled out below with smoke contrails from a space shuttle. In the cab the locomotive has a plaque indicating its historical significance to the space shuttle program. Little Lady has found a good home.

In 2016, the State of Indiana celebrated 200 years of statehood. A torch was carried by foot and other modes of transportation through all 95 counties in the state. From Dupont to North Madison it traveled in style aboard the Madison Railroad Business Car that was in service for the first time since the 1970s and pulled by Engine Number 3. Upon arrival it stopped at the Route 7 highway crossing. This is the exact location where, 180 years ago to the day, the first ground was broken on September 16, 1836, for the Madison and Indianapolis Railroad, the oldest rail line in the state. Several dignitaries accompanied the train and made a few remarks to the citizens assembled. In the hour preceding, music was provided by Steve Jeffries. Remarks were made by a couple of voices from the distant past, an 1840 vintage railroad man and an 1850 vintage Madison glory days railroad president, Ol' John Brough. Four generations of the Fuehring family, including Roger's mom, were on hand to help make it all happen along with Cathy Hale and the entire staff of the Madison Railroad arriving by train with the torch.

Community events are important to Madison Railroad. For several years the employees of Madison Railroad have provided annual Santa Train rides in North Vernon and Madison. One Saturday each year at either end of the railroad you will see over 1,200 kids and adults alike meeting Santa Claus and his helpers as they ride the rails of Indiana's most historic piece of railroad.

This brings us to the year 2018. The Madison Railroad is celebrating 40 years of providing rail service to Jefferson and Jennings counties and the communities therein. Indiana can celebrate in November 2018, the 180th anniversary of the first passenger train to operate in the state on this very line. The original stone arches and culverts over which that first iron horse trod continue to serve unmodified for the most part, and they serve very well. What a bargain, purchased in 1836/1838 during the Internal Improvements era. These stones set one upon another upon another by expert masons still function as intended, even though their builders could not possibly have envisioned the weight and size of 21st century locomotives and cars. Ditto much of the supporting stonework bearing the weight of the rebuilt and refurbished bridges spanning the five major streams between North Madison and North Vernon. The trains roll on.

Crew of Madison Railroad with Locomotive 3 that pulled the bi-centennial train on 9/16/2016. Employees left to right: W. Roger Fuehring, Robert Griffin, Chris Brawner, Cathy Hale, Casey Goode, Terry Fletcher and Ira Sprong. **Photo by Drayton Blackgrove**

PART 5

The Five Major Bridges of the Madison Railroad

THE FIVE MAJOR BRIDGES OF THE MADISON RAILROAD

When the State of Indiana began building the original Madison, Indianapolis and Lafayette Railroad in 1836 from the Ohio River to North Vernon, bridge building had been primarily confined to viaducts based upon the Roman design, arches, trestles and small structures over insignificant streams. Transportation infrastructure, as we call it today, was in the infancy stage. The builders faced a decision at five major stream crossings—stone viaducts, trestles or wooden bridges. Their options were limited by material at hand as well as technology. Timber bridges were chosen. The strength value of the triangle had been determined and in 1820, the lattice truss bridge was patented. By 1836/1839 it had been deemed trustworthy so something like the lattice truss or a later development of it may have been used on the Madison. Due to span length, these timber bridges were likely supported by vertical timber bents. The record is silent as to exactly what type of bridges were original to the property. What is known is the location where all five stream crossings on the Madison Railroad are now. Also known, many stone abutments and wing walls remain where the pioneers placed them 180-years ago.

Why timber for streams instead of stone arches? The stone arches would not be practicable. Primarily, it was what was readily available with vast affordable quantities of timber. The forests of Southern Indiana were adjacent to the right-of-way ready for the cutting making long distance transportation a non-issue. Good quality timber was available and skilled bridge builders and laborers were plentiful. Timber bridges were relatively easy to build, modify and rebuild as necessary.

The downsides of timber were its susceptibility to fire and to washout in floods, the latter due to debris piling behind vertical timber bents in the stream bed. Also, timber deteriorated quickly in the days before wood preservatives were invented. Freshets and floods were common. The less wooden surface touching Indiana soil, or the stream bed, the better. Trestle bents did suffer this infirmity. Therefore, stone abutments as opposed to timber abutments were used at bridge ends. Stone piers were used as intermediate supports when practicable. The wooden superstructure rested on as much solid rock as possible, likely abetted by as few vertical timber bents as possible.

Early design of the Madison and Indianapolis Railroad bridges called for the supporting truss to be under the running surface. Such bridges are called deck trusses. The sides were vertical sheathed like barn siding and the deck was "pitched and caulked." This was to keep the weather from prematurely weakening the structure. A deck truss is opposed to a through truss. Here the train passes through the superstructure rather than over. These may be covered as evidenced by several covered bridges still found on a few roadways in the state.

The photo at right shows a Civil War vintage Howe truss being prepared for demolition in Virginia. No through trusses were ever used on the M&I, only deck trusses.

Good building stone, like good timber, was readily available along the right of way. While quarrying and cutting was more difficult than felling timber, the effort was worth it. Stone does not burn nor does it deteriorate. Contact with solid ground and stream beds is not a problem. In a word, stone is permanent. All five major bridges had limestone abutments, limestone wing walls as necessary and some had stone piers. Abutment stone was smoothed and faced on the horizontal and vertical surfaces where joints in construction were made but left rough on the exposed surface face and

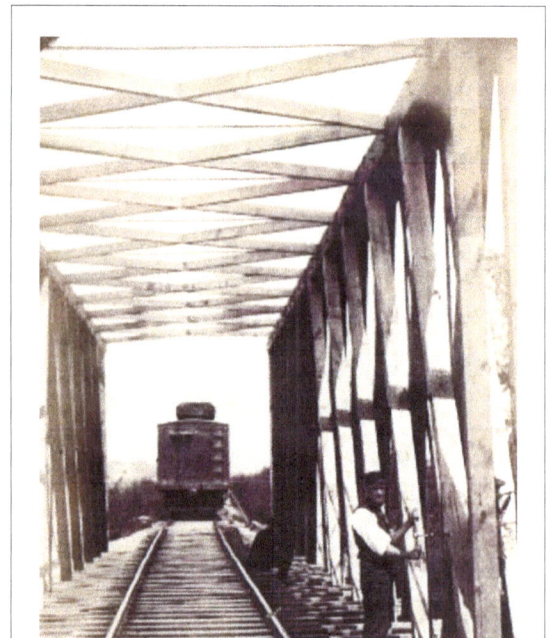

Civil War military personnel drilling preparatory holes to destroy this wooden Howe truss bridge. Andrew J. Russel photo of Railroad operations in Northern Virginia, 1862-1863. **Library of Congress. Prints and Photographs Division.**

the hidden back side. Stone for piers was smoothed on all sides. Many of the original stone works remain in place today, albeit reinforced and surfaced with newer stone or concrete.

Old time bridge builders demanded seasoned timber, air dried for two years. As the railway age picked up speed, this delay became impossible to live with. The Howe truss was patented in 1840 to solve the problem. This breakthrough allowed timber bridges to be built of partly seasoned timber and then adjusted with screws and nuts on connecting iron tension rods to keep joints tight. Iron was much more plentiful in 1840 than 20 years prior. Howe trusses were used on the Madison but it is unknown as to exactly when.

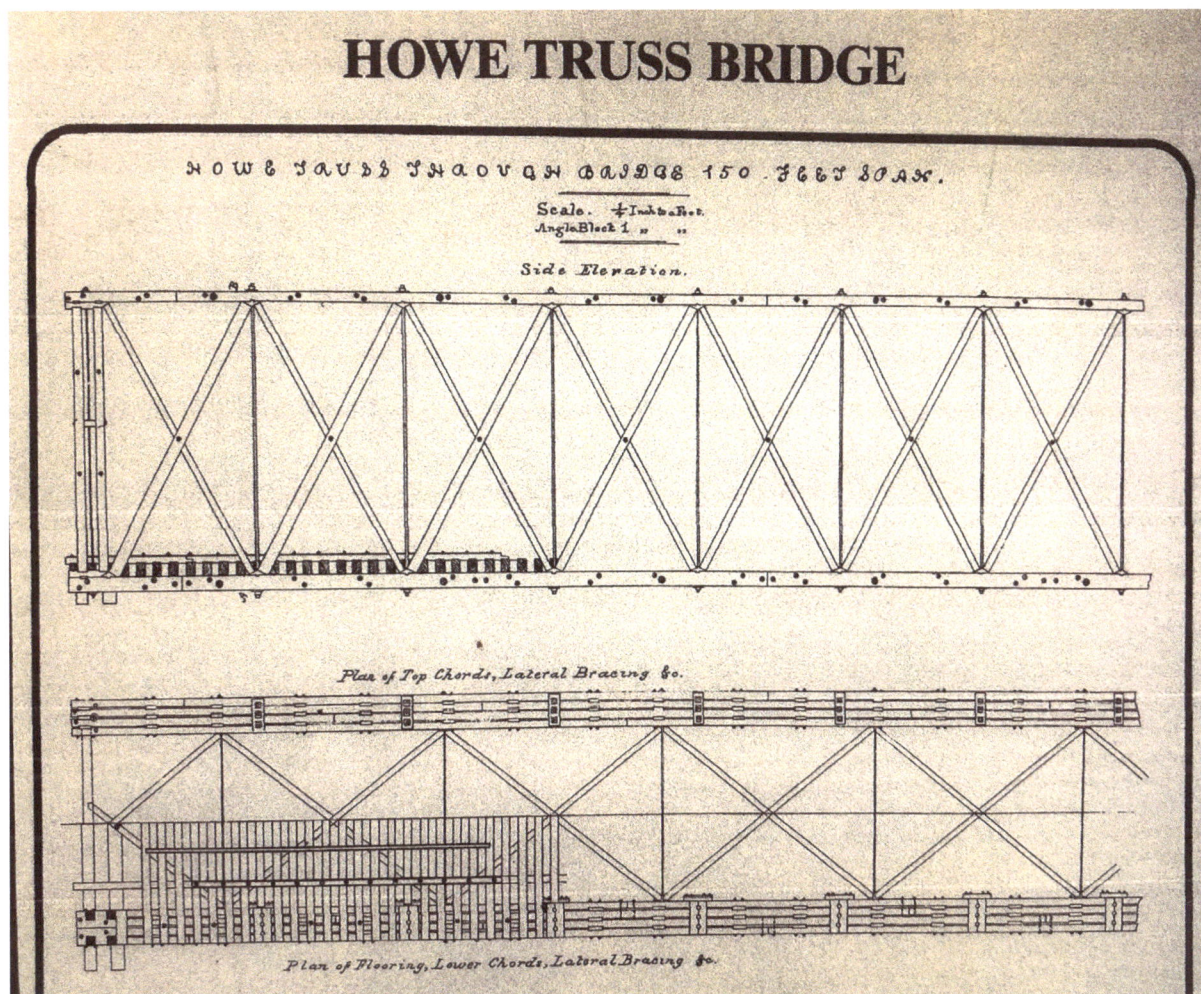

Engineering Sketch of a Howe Truss Bridge

In July of 1863, Confederate General John Hunt Morgan raided his way across Southern Indiana, visiting Vernon, the M&I and Dupont on his way east. He was backed down by the heroic home guard forces at Vernon and so turned to the South. His force was much better known for fire and mayhem than combat. The General severed the rail line in two places by burning the bridges at Graham Creek and Big Creek and possibly damaging others. No doubt the damage was repaired quickly and temporarily by flimsy looking trestles described by President Lincoln as "made of corn stalks and bean poles." The permanent replacements were very likely Howe designs.

Historical marker southeast of Dupont, IN adjacent to a county road. General Morgan inflicted fire and fury on Dupont and the M&I Railroad before plundering on east..
Charlie Wise Collection

General Morgan was a hero in the South and seen as the devil on horseback in the North. He torched and pillaged Dupont breaking up and ruining much of everything not carted off. His damage included, in addition to the two bridges burned, the railroad depot, a warehouse and a twelve car train. His fellow horsemen did cart off about 2,000 hams, some of which soon spoiled in transit in the July heat. This provided a perfect trail by which to follow him east as the aromatic fetid pork was discarded. A stone marker along highway 1050 North, east of Dupont, marks the spot where the Confederates had breakfast on July 12, 1863. Ham was likely on the menu.

It is unclear exactly when the bridges not destroyed by Morgan were replaced with Howe trusses but all five streams were crossed well prior to 1900 by this type of bridge. Iron bridges became more common by 1870, but by this time, the M&I was a minor branch of a much larger system. Iron seems to have been deemed too expensive in the decade after the Civil War. Thus, it is very likely that timber Howe bridges, with a capacity adequate to the traffic, were built and supported with vertical bents as the weight of locomotives and cars increased. All bridges on the Madison built between 1836 and 1900 were new and all were very likely of timber. By 1900, the advantages enjoyed by stick built timber bridges dissipated and steel replacements became advantageous. This was due to overall economy as steel is stronger and lasts much longer. All bridges installed on the Madison after 1900 until 2010 were secondhand steel and re-purposed from main line locations on the then current owner, the Pennsylvania Railroad (PRR). The PRR maintained their bridges very well and three of the five bridges, still today, being well maintained by the Madison Railroad, look much like they did when Penn Central cut the Madison Branch adrift in 1976.

1

The first of the five bridges north of Madison is the Middlefork Bridge at Mile post MP 35.25 as measured from Columbus. There was a small community in this vicinity as shown in photo.

The original bridge at this location was in place by November 1838 for the first train operated with steam power in the state. The present bridge is 180-feet in length, is 71-feet high and consists of three deck plate girder spans supported by two stone/concrete abutments and two intermediate piers, one of steel set on a stone base and the other stone/concrete. In 2010, this bridge received a renewal including concrete work, all new bridge cross ties and steel walkways. It is well painted and well cared for.

The oldest bridge over Middlefork for which there is firm evidence was a Howe truss bridge supported by two stone abutments and by 1911, 10 timber bents. The exact date of construction is unknown, but likely circa 1870. One or more bridges preceded the Howe.

Madison RR predecessor depot facilities at Middlefork, IN. Exact date and photographer unknown.. **Courtesy of the Jefferson County Historical Society.**

Madison Railroad CEO, Cathy Hale, signed the Middlefork concrete work in 2010.

The timber Howe Bridge was replaced in 1911 by the present structure consisting of three used deck plate girder spans re-purposed to this location by PRR. Middlefork is the only bridge on the Madison Railroad with a steel intermediate pier. The 40-foot span came from Three Mile Run near Knightstown, IN. It was built in 1897. One 70-foot span originally crossed Buck Creek near Ogden, IN and was also built in 1897. The other 70-feet span came from Montgomery's Creek, west of Knightstown, IN and was built in 1899. The three secondhand bridge spans became available with much service life remaining, as the main line was upgraded to handle higher speeds, heavier cars, tonnage and locomotives.

There are three generations of masonry visible here. The wing wall appears to date to 1838. Other stonework came later, the exact date unknown, as the, cut, size and color are different. Concrete pier caps and abutment buttressing date to 1911, with repairs as needed made since. It seems highly likely that hidden beneath the "newer" stone and concrete is the original mason's craftsmanship dating to construction days.

Near Madison, IN. Middlefork Creek Bridge, MP 35.25 looking west, downstream. **Charlie Wise Collection**

Middlefork Creek Bridge, looking northwest. Wing wall stone, covered in moss, dates to 1838. Stone and concrete in the north abutment likely cover more 1838 masonry. **Charlie Wise Collection**

Middlefork Creek Bridge, looking southwest at south abutment. Stonemasonry predates the concrete head wall and pedestals by decades. **Charlie Wise Collection**

Middlefork Creek Bridge, looking north/northwest at north pier and showing steel pier, the only one on the Madison Railroad. **Charlie Wise Collection**

2 The next bridge moving north is at MP 33.57 spanning Big Creek. The present bridge, constructed by the Madison Railroad in 2011, is 192-feet long and 73-feet high. This stream was originally spanned by November 1838, as the first train from North Madison to Graham Creek passed over it. The type of bridge built in 1838 and actually, the style and number of bridge replacements, if any, before the Civil War are all unknown. General Morgan destroyed this bridge in July of 1863. The permanent replacement was almost certainly a Howe truss. By 1900, a timber Howe truss bridge had been in service for many years and was ready for replacement. The shift from timber to steel was on.

The PRR once again chose secondhand and found excess three identical spans of a long multi-span structure over Yellow Creek draining into the Ohio River in the bottoms, downstream a few miles from Steubenville, OH. In 1900, one was moved to Big Creek and re-purposed to serve for 111 years. Quoting the PRR bridge plans:

Three identical spans erected at Bridge No. 417 Columbus Division formerly No 3 Indianapolis Division of P. C. C. & St L Ry in 1880 by Keystone Bridge Co. Pittsburgh, Pa. Spans remodeled and erected at present sites in 1900 by Louisville Bridge and Iron Co. File No. F 47-2...Reinforced by Wooden Bents under c and i points in 1920 by Division. File No. F 54-4.

Near Dupont, IN. Big Creek Bridge at MP 33.57. Photo taken during the 2011 rebuilding.
Madison Railroad Collection

In 2009, during a severe flood, a tree lodged against one of the timber bents and damage was done. The line was severed for two weeks. The cost to repair the damage was significant. The decision was made shortly thereafter to completely replace this bridge.

In August 2011 a brand new concrete deck girder bridge was completed. It consists of four spans, each 48-feet long, supported by three free standing piers, two concrete and one stone, concrete clad and enhanced.

This is the first new bridge, scratch built on site, on the Madison Railroad since circa the Civil war when the last of the five timber Howe trusses was completed.

Near Dupont at Big Creek Bridge, 2011 after complete rebuilding, looking southwest, downstream. **Madison Railroad Collection**

Near Dupont, IN, Big Creek Bridge, looking northwest. Several generations of stonemason work, some dating to 1838, accompany the modern concrete. **Madison Railroad Collection**

STEEL WHEELS KEEP ON TURNING.

Bridges are like kids in a way. One is not supposed to pick favorites but Graham Creek is hard to resist among the three steel bridges. The setting is pristine in addition to being historical.

Near Vernon, IN at Graham Creek Bridge, MP 28.60. Looking east, upstream. **Charlie Wise Collection**

3 This location, before the coming of the M&I Railroad, was Graham Ford. The outline of the "road" is still visible. The first revenue train crossed Graham Creek right here on June 6, 1839. Morgan's marauders paid a visit in July of 1863 and things got really hot until the railroad bridge was no more. A temporary structure was no doubt quickly thrown across using the stone work of 1839 on both sides as jumping off points. After all, there was a war on and a war to win.

The present bridge, at MP 28.60, is 280-feet long including jump spans, making it the largest bridge on the Madison Railroad. It is roughly 75-feet high and looks even higher in the forest. The design is a pin deck truss of the Pratt family. It is simply beautiful as bridges go.

The present bridge replaced a Howe truss timber model of unknown age, but likely immediate post-Civil War, courtesy of General Morgan. At time of replacement the Howe had eight timber bents under the main span plus several more under the original timber jump span. The steel truss came from the PRR Ohio River crossing at Steubenville, OH. It was originally the east span on the West Virginia side, installed there in 1887-1888. It is a Pratt truss. At 235-feet, it was too long for Graham Creek when relocated in 1909. No problem. The PRR simply knocked down part of the south abutment several feet lower, made it a free standing pier, and dug out the earth several feet to the south. There they erected a new, much shorter abutment. The used Ohio River span fit right in place to a jump span which attached to mother earth.

An identical jump span is on the north end. Dates of November 1887, have been found marked on the steel near the south end of the Pratt truss. This makes the Graham Creek bridge the oldest of the five.

Near Vernon, IN at Graham Creek Bridge, looking southwest.
Wing wall to the right dates to 1839.
Charlie Wise Collection

The stonemasonry in the abutments and piers date to the 1909 installation of the present structure. No doubt, behind/under this is 1839 stonemason craftsmanship still rock solid. The wing walls likely date to 1839 when the first train went to Vernon on June 6th of that year. Recent improvements include repairs to the south abutment and some concrete repair to other stone work. Graham Creek, like all steel bridges, was pressure washed in the 1990s. It received adequate coats of linseed oil paint at that time. As I said—looking good, top to bottom.

Near Vernon at Graham Creek on topside, looking north.
Charlie Wise Collection

Near Vernon at Graham Creek Bridge, looking east, upstream.
Charlie Wise Collection

4 Next is the South Fork of the Muscatatuck River. The original survey in 1836 laid out the MI&L crossing two forks of the Muscatatuck River about one quarter mile above their union. Still the same pattern today. The first revenue train crossed here on June 6, 1839. The South Fork Bridge is at MP 23.33. The present structure is 144-feet long, the shortest bridge on the Madison Railroad and 83-feet high, making it the tallest of the five bridges. It consists of three 48-feet spans, concrete deck girder, with two free standing concrete piers. No jump spans to solid ground account for it being shorter than the others.

Near Vernon at the South Fork of the Muscatatuck River Bridge at MP 23.32, looking northwest, downstream. Bridge completely rebuilt by Madison Railroad in 2011. Here, modern concrete co-exists with ancient stonemasonry, dating to 1839. **Charlie Wise Collection**

Near Vernon at South Fork of the Muscatatuck River Bridge, looking northwest. **Charlie Wise Collection**

The masonry at South Fork is very interesting. Four generations are on full display here. 1839 rough cut stone abutments and wing wall, later cut smoothed stone bridge seat pedestals, concrete reinforcing to the head walls of the abutments and finally, the shiny modern concrete of 2011.

Near Vernon at the South Fork of the Muscatatuck River Bridge. An 1839 southeast wing wall and stonehead wall abutment, concrete upright pedestal, set on circa 1900 masonry. 1839 to 2011, side-by-side, within just a few dozen feet. **Charlie Wise Collection**

The bridge and a concrete structure replaced was identical to the one described in connection with Big Creek. The two spans were 131-year-old twins when replaced, identical even to the timber trestles adding support after 1920.

Near Vernon at the South Fork of the Muscatatuck River Bridge before the 2011 rebuilding. Timber trestle support added by PRR in 1920 to strengthen the structure. **Madison Railroad Photo.**

Near Vernon at the South Fork of the Muscatatuck River Bridge. Locomotive 3634 pulling a transformer over the bridge in 2015.
Madison Railroad Collection

Near Vernon at the South Fork of the Muscatatuck River Bridge looking west, downstream. **Madison Railroad Collection**

5 Last in line of the five bridges and closest to Vernon is the bridge over the North Fork of the Muscatatuck River at MP 23.19. This site is the easiest to access by vehicle. The present modified Pratt truss has been in place since 1906. It is 189-feet long, counting jump span, and 78-feet high. It is very well maintained, painted and pressure washed in the 1990's by the Madison Railroad.

The first revenue train crossed here and then rolled on into Vernon on June 6, 1839.

Near Vernon at the North Fork of the Muscatatuck River Bridge at MP. 23.19, looking east, upstream.
Charlie Wise Collection

Near Vernon at the North Fork of the Muscatatuck River Bridge, looking southeast.
Charlie Wise Collection

Prior to this current structure, a timber Howe truss was in place. When it was constructed is unknown but by 1906, its time to go had arrived. Again, the PRR decided on secondhand replacement instead of scratch-built for the task. Another excess span from the multi-span Yellow Creek, Ohio Bridge, in the Ohio River bottoms flood plain, supplied the need for the Madison Branch. It was disassembled, loaded up and hauled to Southern Indiana. This span dates to 1890, but the pedigree is not quite as clear as is with Graham Creek, marked in steel, "1887" for example. No dates have been discovered on any of the structural members.

This bridge has no center pier like Middlefork has. Trusses allow for longer span clear length than deck plate girders. The south end consists of an abutment showing three generations of stone work.

Most impressive are the parapets atop the curved wing wall, all dating from 1839. The steel structure rests upon 1906 stone work. Above that is bright white concrete applied by the Madison Railroad in recent years. The freestanding pier between the main span and the jump span is 1906 vintage stonemasonry repaired as needed.

Near Vernon at the North Fork of the Muscatatuck River Bridge, looking southeast, showing the steel pin truss construction and 1839 stonemasonry to include a delightfully curved fender.
Charlie Wise Collection

Many years ago, the railroad numbered their bridges instead of designating them by milepost. The North Fork of The Muscatatuck was Bridge 201.

North Fork Muscatatuck River Bridge, topside, looking south. Photographer and exact date unknown. Likely circa 1900. PRR numbered bridges in lieu of milepost numbers. This is Bridge 201 per sign on left. Note: the man in the photo was apparently trespassing, thus putting himself in danger, ironically not far from the NO TRESPASSING sign to the right. **Photo Courtesy of the Jeffersonville Historical Society**

PART 6

The Stone Arches of the Madison Railroad

The Stone Arches Of The Madison Railroad

Oh, those arches, those stone arch bridges and culverts! Ancient and solid workmanship of the mason. Every railroad has bridges, but not every railroad has arches. There are 23 active miles and one and three quarter inactive miles on the Madison Railroad. Here we find 10 Romanesque major stone arches, all but one over a stream and 20 smaller box culverts.

Madison, IN Crooked Creek Arch, looking west.
Charlie Wise Collection

Near Dupont, IN. 1838 vintage box culvert at MP 33.95 alongside Middlefork Road beneath the Madison Railroad.
Charlie Wise Collection

They all date to 1837-1838. This is the largest cluster of such structures in the state of Indiana and all were built by the state of Indiana. In a progress report dated 1839 to the officials in Indianapolis, the writer stated the following: "Streams of a larger nature requiring greater waterway—and yet not so large as to require a timber bridge (are crossed) by means of arched culverts formed of substantial stone masonry and varying in their span from 6 to 30 feet." Sadly, no names of the master stonemasons were included.

Prior to 1850, few arches were built by the railroads due to initial cost. The normal procedure was to build on the cheap—timber and dirt—get something up and running, and then improve it later as business volume produced revenue. A fine example of this strategy was the Mad River and Lake Erie Railroad, an Ohio pioneer line. It came to be about the same time as the MI&L . By 1838, 15 miles of wobbly strap rail and ties atop the contours of mother earth were completed between Sandusky and Bellevue. The only thing on this line that was first class was the one locomotive, the SANDUSKY. The MI&L on the other hand, was built to

Vernon, IN. Northwest quadrant of the Vernon Pike Street Stone Arch at MP 22.90, showing the large retaining wall in place since 1837. **Charlie Wise Collection**

first-class standards, top to bottom. That initial investment is still paying dividends 180 years later.

Arches are very strong by design and due to distribution of stress, get stronger under load. They also provide a huge, unobstructed opening to handle colossal floods.

Only one has ever failed. See next section for details. All arches were and are constructed of stone and all 9 on the 23 active miles are basically in as built condition. Arches have a very long life expectancy. They just never wear out. Some are lined with brick to protect the barrel stone from water damage. Others are not lined. The brick linings may or may not be original. On that point the record is silent.

Madison Crooked Creek Arch (again), looking west. Opening large enough to handle 15" of rain runoff but not large enough to allow complete houses etc., to pass through, thus forming a dam. The 1863 rebuilt arch is a perfect copy of the 1841 arch that washed away in the flood.

Charlie Wise Collection

The Vernon Arch, MP 22.90 from Columbus, is by far the easiest to access. You can drive through it unless you are in a very high vehicle. It crosses Pike Street in this delightfully preserved community, populated by very nice people and comprised of scads of historic structures. The Jennings County Courthouse is nearby as is the Jennings County Historical society. An ancient building with massive stone walls right next to the arch is reported to be the original depot.

Vernon, looking east, along Pike Street toward the Vernon Arch (far left out of photo). Drugstore on corner is now the Jennings County Historical Society. The four story building, far left, is reported to be the M&I depot. It may be the oldest depot still standing in the state of Indiana. **Photo courtesy of the Jefferson County Historical Society.**

Vernon, looking east, at Pike Street Arch. Arch and depot to the far right (outside of photo) are still standing in 2018. Photographer and exact date unknown, but likely circa 1900. **Photo courtesy of the Jefferson County Historical Society.**

Vernon 1837 Pike Street Arch looking west. This is the oldest grade separation structure west of the Appalachians.
Charlie Wise Collection

The Vernon Arch may be the prettiest of the lot as well. It's parapets, abutments and massive curved wing wall on the east side and the marvelous retaining wall on the west side give testament to the aesthetic awareness of the builder. The stone plaque over the arch on the west side is largely illegible now due to weathering, but what can be read is as follows: "BUILT BY ...D. Pallentine...1837".

Mr. Pallentine and his men did an admirable job indeed building this first railroad/highway grade separation west of the Appalachians.

The Vernon Arch is 28-feet deep, has a 16-foot span and is 12-feet high. It was built large enough to accommodate the second track over the street serving the depot facilities.

Vernon Pike Street Arch. Inscription stone above apex of the arch on the west side that is very badly deteriorated. The parts that can be deciphered are: " BUILT BY....D. Pallentine...1837.
Charlie Wise Collection

Vernon looking topside to the north of Pike Street Arch. Switch above arch leads to the depot and terminal building and maybe to the ancient turntable behind the photographer to the Left. Photographer and date unknown. Likely circa 1900.
Photo courtesy of Jefferson County Historical Society

The entire alignment was needed to gain elevation from the Muscatatuck River crossings while holding the grade to three quarters of one percent. The stone may have come from a quarry at MP 23.75. The arch has a brick lining which has required a bit of maintenance from time to time. Falling bricks are never a good thing. The costs have been very reasonable, averaging $3125 per year over 40 years. It passed all load tests. It is a mighty fine arch indeed.

Vernon Pike Street Arch, looking east.
Charlie Wise Collection

Vernon Pike Street Arch with the last locomotive used on the Incline. Locomotive 3634, southbound in 1996.
Photo courtesy of the Jefferson County Historical Society

To the south of the Muscatatuck River Bridges are three stone arch culverts, all of which are significantly more difficult to reach than the Pike Street structure. The first is located at MP 27 and is called the Mile Post 27 Arch. Concrete Mile Post 27, installed by the PRR alongside the track many decades ago, is now inside the arch. How, why and when it got there is anyone's guess. The structure is an 8-feet wide, 8- feet high, approximately 30-feet deep stone arch.

Near Vernon, IN at MP 27. Arch looking west. How exactly MP 27 migrated from the right of way above to inside the barrel of the arch is unknown. Roger Fuehring uses it to maintain dry footing while exploring the interior of the barrel.
Charlie Wise Collection

Near Vernon at MP.27 Arch, looking southwest. **Charlie Wise Collection**

Next is Mule Pass Arch at MP 27.85. The reason for the name (as one assumes) is the location for mule teams to pass between the once undisturbed valley, now split in two. It is 6-feet wide, 8-feet high and approximately 30-feet deep. There is a spring in the center that locals claim is safe to drink. The last of these three is at MP 29.19. It has a span of 12-feet, 6 inches.

Near Vernon at Mule Pass Arch at MP 27.85, looking east. Named for its use for passing live stock under the M&I Railroad since the late 1830s. A spring is found near the center of the barrel in small offshoot that is reported to have good clean spring water. **Charlie Wise Collection**

Near Vernon at Mule Pass Arch, looking southeast. **Charlie Wise Collection**

Near Vernon at Mule Pass Arch, looking southeast.
Charlie Wise Collection

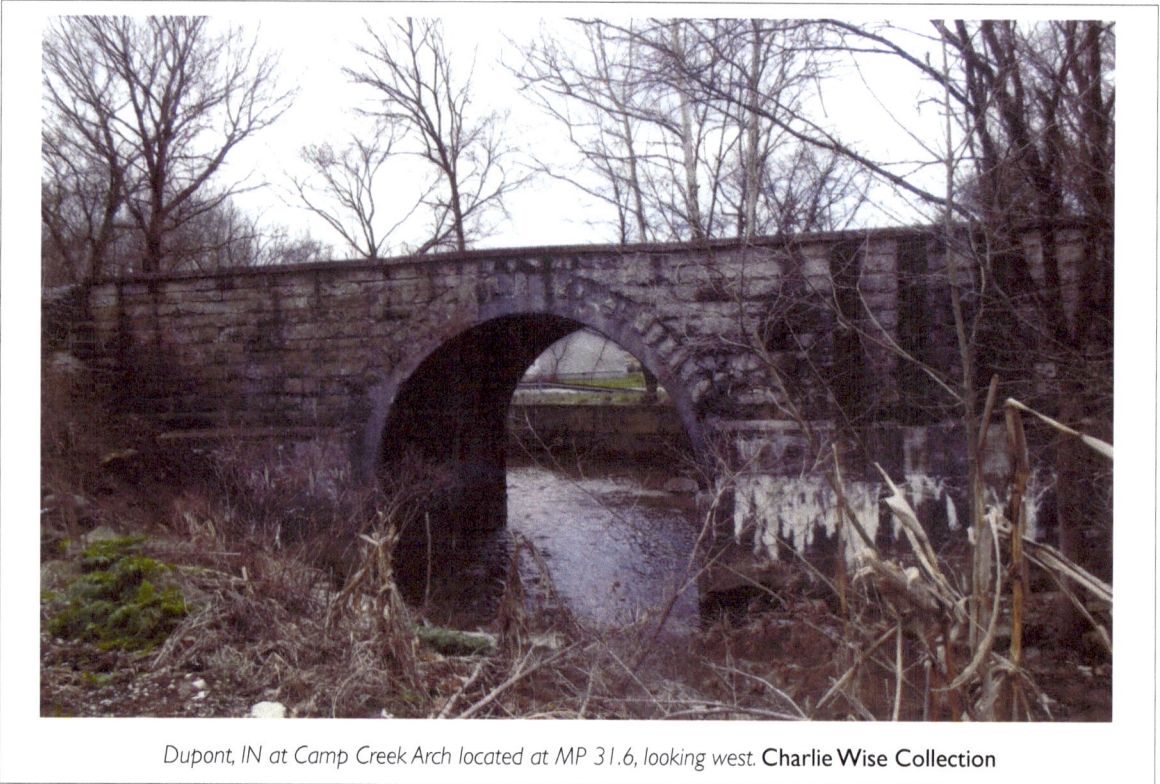

Dupont, IN at Camp Creek Arch located at MP 31.6, looking west. **Charlie Wise Collection**

Just north of the main road crossing in Dupont at MP 31.6 spanning Camp Creek is Dupont Arch. General Morgan burned and pillaged much of Dupont in the summer of 1863. The arch was not well suited for either and stands strong to this day. It is 29-feet deep, possibly designed for two tracks, with a 23-feet span. It is 13-feet high over the normal creek level. It has fine parapets and stone abutments, the latter buttressed by decades old concrete at the base. The vertical draw timbers abetting the north abutment were put in place in the 1990s. After that it load tested just fine for heavy rolling stock.

Dupont, IN at Camp Creek Arch located at MP 31.6. Looking northwest, showing large timbers to reinforce abutments on the upstream side. Timbers applied in the 1990s. **Charlie Wise Collection**

Dupont Arch at Camp Creek, looking east with business car legacy passing over. **Photo Courtesy of North Vernon Plain Dealer. Photo by Bryce Mayer.**

Dupont, IN, looking east (upstream) at Camp Creek Arch. **Charlie Wise Collection**

The barrel is brick lined. Some significant repairs were made during the 1990s. Included were grouting and concrete facing. Costs for the Dupont Arch have been a reasonable average of $4,375 per year for 40 years. For a good view, drive along the road on the west side, downstream end. On the opposite side of the road from the arch, once there was a spur from the railroad to a creek side lumber mill. No trace now.

The easiest box culvert to access and photograph is located along the county road, east side, north of Middlefork. It measures to a 3-foot opening surrounded by solid stone work, located at MP 33.8, built 1837 or 1838. It has been there untouched ever since. The rest of the stone culverts up and down the line not converted to pipe/concrete etc., are similar. As is often heard, if you have seen one, you have seen them all. The importance of these little rascals should not be ignored though. In times of wet weather, combined, they all safely carry away a lot of water.

Near Dupont is one of the many similar stone box culverts dating to the early days of railroad building in the state. This one is found at MP 33.95 alongside Middle Creek Road. **Charlie Wise Collection**

Next we come to the Secret Arch or the Wirt Arch spanning Harberts Creek at MP 38.29. It is a secret because access to it is nigh impossible. It is hard to find for the arch is in a very isolated location adjacent to the former Army Jefferson Proving Ground. This site is now home to the Madison Railroad. The arch is a hidden gem in the woods.

As original construction started at North Madison and worked north, this was very likely the first and therefore the oldest major arch built on the railroad. Wirt was completed in 1837. It was definitely the first of the ten major arches to feel the weight of a locomotive pulling a train in November 1838.

The stonemasons produced a span 21-feet long, 22-feet deep and 14-feet high. It is lined with brick. The west side, the downstream side, is very well preserved in all regards to include parapets and abutment supports. Some concrete lower face buttressing has been applied on the south abutment. Other than this, it is in as built condition.

Near Jefferson Proving Ground (Wirt) is Harberts Creek Arch at MP38.39. This is the oldest arch on the Madison Railroad and the oldest in the state based upon the construction pattern followed by the original MI&L builders that broke ground at North Madison and worked north. Harberts Creek was the first major stream encountered. **Photo by Roger Fuehring**

The east side has needed some major work. When the JPG was built, the Army diverted the creek, changing the course, direction, angle of current and force of flow against the south buttress. The Secret Arch's original east side wing wall on the south bank was washed away and the north bank wing wall was in poor condition. Over the decades after the 1940s, erosion took its toll as it had not done before.

To protect and preserve the structure for another 180 years, the largest repair to any arch on the Madison Railroad was accomplished in 2017. This project involved some stonemasonry removal and some being encased in the massive new concrete wing walls. These were built to divert the creek back to its original flow path. The arch itself remain as originally built and stone strong going forward.

Near JPG (Wirt) at Harberts Creek Arch, looking east. Referred to at times as the Secret Arch based on its inaccessibility. **Madison Railroad Collection**

Moving on south are three smaller arches in North Madison. The first is just south of RTE 62 behind a dental office, so it is named the Dentist Office Arch. It is pretty well citified as opposed to the rural pristine examples to the north. It has a 6-foot span with a sewer pipe running through it. Lots of concrete on the west side obscures the stone work underneath. The recently fallen Sycamore tree further blocks the view of this arch.

Near JPG at Harberts Creek Arch, looking west. **Charlie Wise Collection**

Harberts Creek Arch near JPG After new wing walls have been installed on the east side in 2017. What was left of the original 1837 wing walls encased into the new wing walls. Original arch still remains intact. **Photo by Roger Fuehring**

Next at MP 41.89 is a diminutive arch not citified. It is adjacent to Wilson Avenue. The 8-foot wide Wilson Avenue Arch, with its solid lines and buttressing, is a tiny example of the aesthetic sense of proportion possessed by the ancient masons.

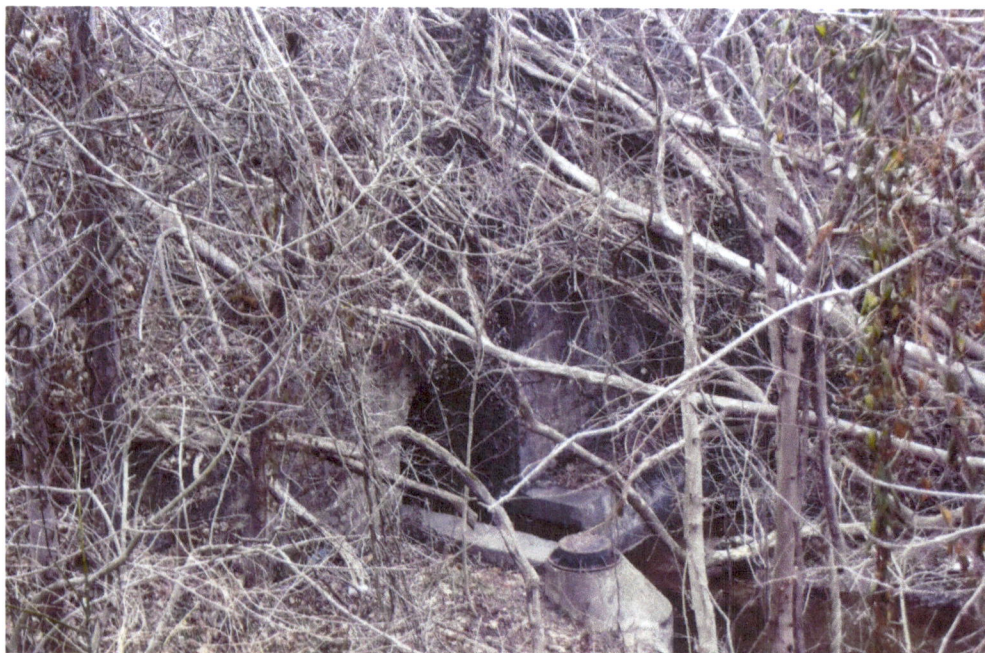

Near North Madison just south of SR 62 at MP 41.38. View of arch outlet is obstructed by a fallen Sycamore tree. **Photo by Charlie Wise.**

Near North Madison, north of Wilson Avenue at MP 41.69, looking west. **Charlie Wise** Collection

The last of the active portion arches on the Madison Railroad is located at MP 42.1. It originally was a double–two, 3-foot arches. Now it has two cast iron pipe cores. This double arch culvert is located behind a mobile home community at Wilson and Banta Avenues so is named the Trailer Park Arch.

The tenth arch, the granddaddy of them all, the Crooked Creek Arch and the Madison Incline, demand a separate section.

North Madison at MP 42.1, looking east, located on the backside of a mobile home community. One of several double barreled arch's with upgraded iron pipe. **Charlie Wise** Collection

PART 7

The Big Hill and the Big Arch

The Big Hill and the Big Arch

For being a relatively small town, Madison boasts two very large and very old engineering accomplishments. From the top of the hill in North Madison to the riverfront in Madison lies the Madison Incline. Just up that big hill, near the highway overpass at the west edge of Madison is the Big Arch, or more accurately, the Crooked Creek Arch. Both were conceived in the mid 1830's. The incline at 5.89% grade is the steepest non cog mainline railway grade in the United States. The hill is the first significant railroad grade (over 1%) built in the state of Indiana. The Big arch is one of the largest and longest standing such structures in the Old Northwest. Both were originally built by the state and later the arch was rebuilt after an epic flood. Two relatively hidden gems in plain sight in beautiful Madison, Indiana.

Madison, IN Postcard. P. C. C. & ST. L. Railroad cut card, printed in Madison and postmarked September, 1913.
Charlie Wise Collection

The Madison Incline, aka The Big Hill, was by far the most challenging and most expensive section of the MI&L Railroad to construct. It took five years to complete, in part due to typography and in part due to personal slovenliness and chicanery on the part of some contractors. Ultimately the honest ones finished the task, a task taking longer than necessary. Jacksonian Era civil engineering technology provided few tools to the builders. Black powder, scrapers, wheel barrows, draft animals and hundreds of human laborers did the work. By today's standards, it was built by hand, Irish hands. There were plenty of Irish hands willing to work long and very hard for relatively little pay, plus some whiskey of questionable pedigree. In those days the Irish were not well thought of in the USA by those who came over the pond ahead of them. Bigotry was common and accepted. The Irish took any job they could find. Railroad building was one of these. Coast to coast, our country's railroad network is blanketed with the works of the Irish. Few are more massive and fewer yet are older than these two in Madison.

The Incline is roughly one mile and a half long, rising 413 feet. The entire tangent is either on a fill or in a cut. Much of the spoil excavated from the cuts was used to construct the fills. The Big Cut is 1150-feet long, 40-feet wide and at one point, 125-feet deep. This cut alone provided one quarter million tons of earth and rock.

The other cuts on the Incline added another quarter million tons to bring the total to 500,000 tons moved by horse and by hand. Local tradition in Madison has long held that St. Michael's Catholic Church, constructed by Irish stonemasons who were similarly engaged in building the Madison Incline, is composed of stones excavated from the cuts on the Incline. In 2014 this was called into question. Sarah Ward and Robert Wolfe, writing for the Heritage Trail Conservancy in Madison state: "Research by historic Madison Inc. has found this (source of the stone) to be untrue. The stone for St. Michael's Catholic Church came from a quarry in the northeast section of the city." Regardless, bless the Irish for all their hard work in building Madison landmarks that remain to this day.

Picture taken from Hanging Rock Hill on SR 7, looking at MP 43.34 on the out of service incline to the west, through the trees.
Charlie Wise Collection

In addition to cutting and filling, a few small stone stream crossings were installed on the incline to control run off. They are still there, functioning as intended and as sound as the day the Irish handled the stone work.

By late 1841, the Big Hill and the Big Arch were ready for trains. Contrary to often stated opinion, it appears that at least one (maybe two) early day train(s) with an adhesion locomotive came down the hill and made it back up just fine. *The Madison Courier* on 11/06/1841, reported that, "in the morning a locomotive, unnamed, and a burthen (freight) car, left the riverfront. Aboard were the former Governor Noble and other dignitaries plus about everyone who could find a place to hang on, the latter numbering 80 to 100. The trip to North Madison was made successfully in about 11 minutes. After this, regular service commenced but without locomotives. Cars were let down the hill by gravity and returned to North Madison by teams of horses."

Small culvert in service since 1841 on the 5.89% incline in Madison. **Charlie Wise Collection**

Apparently this use of animals did not prove satisfactory to management. In 1845, the Baldwin Locomotive Works of Philadelphia built engine DE WITT CLINTON. It was able to handle only two cars on the incline. This also proved unacceptable so the locomotive was disposed of to another line or possibly renamed. The record examined is silent on this point. Next came the cog engines. This system involved a rack in the middle of the track and a rotating toothed gear on the locomotive. When engaged, the cog crawled up the hill. This proved more successful than the adhesion engine DE WITT CLINTON but the cog system was plagued with maintenance issues and failures. Two cog engines were procured. The M.G. BRIGHT came on line in November 1847 and the MARION was converted to cog and named JOHN BROUGH in May 1850. The real live John Brough never was shy about the use of his name.

Rack engines could take a passenger train up in 20 minutes and freight train up in 25 minutes if all went as planned. In April 1860, a passenger train consisting of 15 cars ascended the hill with three locomotives. The JOHN BROUGH was positioned near the middle of the consist and an adhesion locomotive was on both the head end and the rear end. This triple-header blasting uphill through the Big Cut had to be a sight and a sound to behold.

Master mechanic, Reuben Wells, deciding the cog system had to go, developed an adhesion engine with 10 driving wheels that conquered the 5.89 % challenge. The locomotive named, REUBEN WELLS, began service in July 1868 and was able to handle a passenger train up the hill in five and a half minutes and eight freight cars up in 13 minutes. In 1888, the ten driving wheels were reduced to eight to reduce binding in the curves at the riverfront. After serving for nearly four decades, the REUBEN WELLS was preserved and is presently safely displayed at the Children's Museum in Indianapolis. As the years went by, wood for fuel gave way to coal and steam power gave way to diesel power. The last hill engine, the 3634, is still in service on the Madison Railroad.

Accidents on the Big Hill were few, but anyone with a respect for and an understanding of gravity had to view the down trip as a potentially wild-ride. On November 4, 1845, Conductor Lodge let his passenger car down the hill using the hand brake. Before he reached Madison, a freight car was released from North Madison, against his specific order. The freight brakeman lost control of his charge. The collision resulted in the death of Conductor Lodge. Nearly 100 years later on October 25, 1943, the down train with 12 cars hit wet leaves on the rails. This run away was quickly sliding wildly, in spite of the best efforts of the crew to control it. The pileup at the foot of the hill resulted in one onboard fatality. The wreck train coming down the hill to provide relief also ran away and wrecked when striking the original pileup. Thankfully, no one on the relief train incident was killed, but explaining all this to the boss had to be very difficult .

The Big Hill was shut down by the PRR on January 21, 1959, due to heavy rain and washouts. It was thought it would be abandoned, however, that did not happen and on May 26, 1960 the PRR restored service to the Madison riverfront. Penn Central tried to simply walk away from the Big Hill and Big Arch 1976, but that effort was ultimately thwarted when the Madison Railroad was born despite Penn Central's attempt to abandoned the entire line.

In 1992, the Indiana Kentucky power generating station in Madison received new generating equipment by rail.

When this business was concluded, the Big Hill was shut down and mothballed. The grade, arch and culverts are all in place. Rail and ties are in place as well but, presently unfit for service due to significant erosion and slippage of a section of fill due to water flowing.

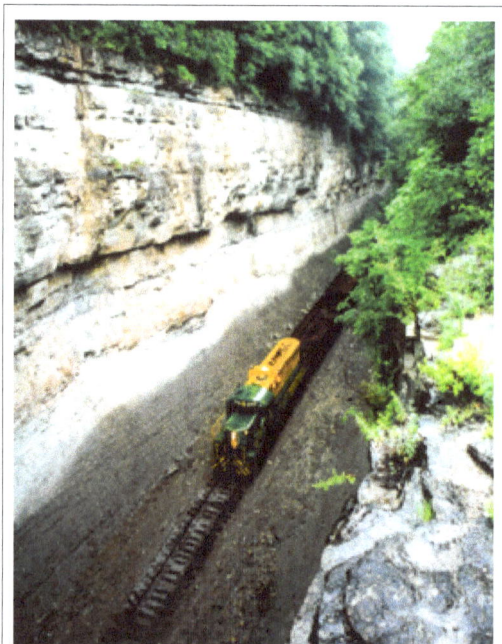

Last shipment down the Incline in 1992. Locomotive 3634 has served on Madison Railroad almost twice as long as it did on the Southern Pacific Railroad, which it was built for.
Photo by Rodney Kelley

The Incline makes for a nice walk but extreme caution should be exercised. Doing so downhill is somewhat less taxing than the reverse.

Near the bottom of the incline, near Main Street, Madison, is the Crooked Creek Stone Arch Bridge. The exact location is MP 43.76, miles from Columbus. Crossing Crooked Creek, this arch is the last major stream crossing on the extant portion of the original MI&L RR. What a grand finale it is. The creme de la creme or the pick of the litter if one prefers. The Crooked Creek Arch barrel is 24-feet side to side, 23-feet, 10-inch in the creekbed, to keystone and 150-feet deep. The track is on a huge fill towering over the waterway approximately 75 feet. This was all originally constructed using early 19th century techniques.

Construction of the arch began in 1837 and was nearly completed by 1838. Contractors Stough and Flint did their job well and in a timely manner. Not so for other portions of the work awarded to multiple contractors. Due to slovenliness and chicanery, some lagged behind. Soon Stough and Flint got more work assisting with the completion of the remainder of the Incline, which included the Crooked Creek Fill. By November 1841, all was in readiness for revenue service. Time for a return on the huge investment and together the passengers and freight came off the Old Michigan Road and on to the railroad. Sadly, at

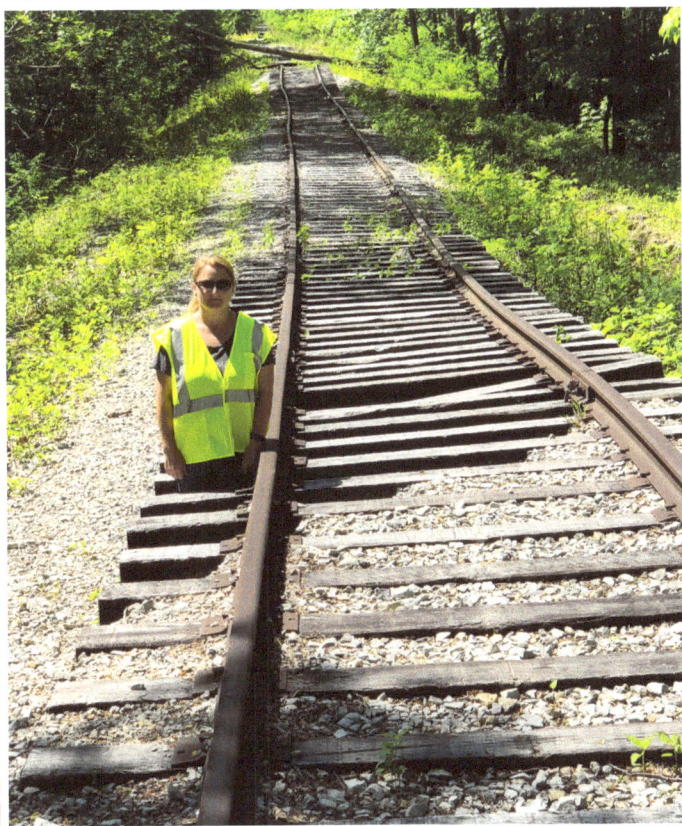

Original MI&L Incline looking south at near the bottom cut at track damage due to slippage and subsidence of the ancient fill. Administrative Manager, Casey Goode demonstrates the extent of the damage. **Photo by Roger Fuehring.**

the same time, the state had run out of money, the railroad had run out of steam, times were tumultuous and northward progress stopped—dead in its tracks.

As the financials improved and private entrepreneurs once again progressed well in the North toward the State Capital, tragedy struck in Madison with what would be called today the 1,000 year flood in the Crooked Creek watershed. Stough and Flint built the MI&L arch well enough to handle the volume of water. However, floods are usually more complicated than a simple 15-inch rain fall. Eleven people lost their lives in this catastrophe. Whole houses, out-buildings, trees and brush all floated downstream and wedged into the barrel of the arch.

MI&L 1841 Incline looking up the 5.89% grade, looking north.
Charlie Wise Collection

Crooked Creek Arch, aka Big Arch in Madison at MP 43.76, looking west. **Charlie Wise Collection**

A dam quickly formed and a lake was impounded by the huge debris mass which likely made a bad situation even worse. When the pressure on the debris dam, arch and fill became unbearable, something had to give. That something was the fill and arch. The washout produced a gaping void 65-feet deep below the rails and 150-feet long. The result was the "total destruction of the arch." This last quote is open to reasonable debate and definition of "total" but the result of the September 3, 1846 flood was obvious. The railroad was severed near the point of its beginning before it reached the end point of its desire, Indianapolis.

Monetary priorities were set previously. Funds were not available to rebuild the stone arch and fill in kind and simultaneously continue construction toward "The Village at The End of the Road." The solution was the quick and relatively cheap construction of a wooden trestle to span the breech in the Madison Incline. The gap was closed in about two weeks by N. C. Barnum at a modest cost of $2,060. Construction work went on toward Indianapolis relatively unimpeded. The 1846 washout, the only arch on the line in 180 years to suffer significant flood damage, was likely a factor in the decision a few years later to attempt a bypass away from the entire incline problem. The result of this was a lot of futile blasting, digging and tunneling in the valley of Clifty Creek producing Brough's Folly. A great deal of arch and fill could have been rebuilt with the $309,000 squandered on that failed effort.

In 1914, long after the folly was abandoned, the PRR revived the idea but quickly dropped it. In 1992 the Big Hill and the Big Arch felt the trod of the last train. It is all still there, intact, though a bit ragged.

After the folly idea was discarded, attention turned to the replacement of the 1846 trestle, likely rebuilt once or more by the time of *The War Between the States*. The flood had taken out or severely damaged about 75-to-100 yards of arch and fill, nearly the length of a football field. By 1859, the solution was obvious as was the need. The time to be rid of the trestle and go back to stone had arrived. Following exactly the plans of 1837, The Crooked Creek Arch was rebuilt. Obviously the pioneers of the age of Jackson, Stough and Flint, did it right. Usable portions of the old arch were simply built upon. According to the M&I annual report: "About 2,400 yards of stonemasonry laid in the most durable manner," was involved by 1863. The work took some time as funding slowly became available. An 1862, capstone dating the edifice was placed but sadly, it has been lost to history. Finally in 1863, at a cost of about

Madison's Big Arch and track atop fill, looking west.
Charlie Wise Collection

$16,000, Madison was reconnected to the rest of the line in a proper manner, by the solid stone arch which remains after 155 years and counting. No trace of the trestle remains.

The Madison Railroad still technically owns the line and arch but with the cessation of service south of the Madison State Hospital switch at North Madison in 1992, little need for track and arch inspections and attention exists. The first recent analysis of the condition of the Crooked Creek Arch came in 2011. It was performed by James E. Adams, PhD of the University of Toledo. He found it basically sound. Dr. Adams noted that the wing walls have a 45-degree angle vs. the more common 30-degree angle.

Big Arch in Madison, looking west. Hard to believe that sleepy, little Crooked Creek caused such damage in the monstrous 1846 flood.
Charlie Wise Collection

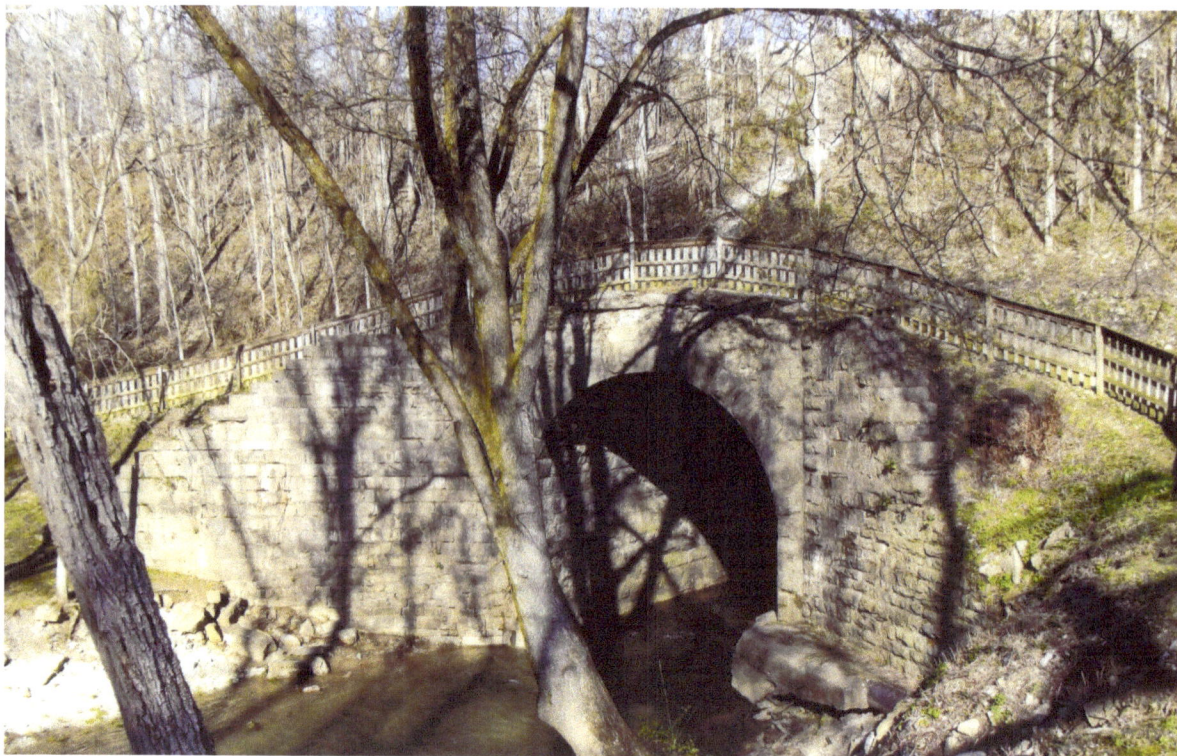

Madison's Big Arch, looking northeast. **Charlie Wise Collection**

The southwest and northwest wing walls, downstream or outlet end, were repaired before the 1846 flood. This would indicate they survived the deluge. According to Dr. Adams, the greatest enemy to the arch is drip seep moisture, not another flood. This arch does not have brick lining. The mortar over all, including inside the barrel needs to be re-pointed. Much of this is cosmetic vs structural and the arch is in no immediate danger.

Madison's Crooked Creek Arch (Big Arch) looking northeast from small park. Much of the original arch washed away in the disastrous flood of 1846. The present Structure is an exact copy of the original. **Charlie Wise Collection**

Madison's Big Arch. This is by Far the largest arch on the Madison Railroad. Photo is of the west side from a small park. Above the water level, about 60' is the track structure. Originally laid out by the MI&L Railroad and opened in 1841.
Charlie Wise Collection

In summer 2014 an exhaustive study was completed and a report rendered to the *Heritage Trail Conservancy*. Titled *HISTORIC STRUCTURE REPORT- STONE ARCH CULVERT-MADISON INCLINE* by Sarah Ward and Robert Wolfe, details were explored fully. Highlights include: "the fills are primarily earth and rock spoil sourced up the hill and are in good shape. The stone faces are unfinished like many of the other arches on the Madison Railroad." Echoing Dr. Adams, Ward and Wolfe agreed that the parapets are pretty much missing and trees and vegetation threaten the wing walls. Graffiti and the concrete encased storm sewer pipe mar the inside of the barrel and the latter provides a walkway enabling the former. Most of the attention required is cosmetic. The overall condition of this 155-year old structure from another age and time is excellent. It is a rare gem indeed. Their sincerely stated desire is to keep it for all to enjoy and explore various action plans to that end.

The Madison Incline, the Big Arch and the Big Hill, in care of the Madison Railroad is in good, capable and intelligent hands. Everyone involved recognizes the gem, the role it has played in history for 180 years and the need for preservation. All is well.

THIS BOOK....

... is dedicated as a capstone to the 40 years of history of the Madison Railroad. It also caps the 182 years since construction began at North Madison, Indiana and celebrates all those who fought to keep her alive and breathing when it appeared all hope was lost. The interesting thing about a row of dominoes, much like history, is if any one domino is missing, it simply stops. The history of so many railroads did just that, stopped. So many times during the history of Indiana's first railroad there were multiple opportunities for all to be lost. The dominoes were all in place from the 1830's until that pivotal day when a fax machine in a little red caboose office rang out. The news was joyously announced: Seventeen miles of track and a 10,000 square foot engine house/office complex building would soon bring stability to the little railroad that could and can. All so perfect. When the ringing stopped and the fax machine moved to its tones and beeps, it spit out a single page. WE GOT IT! With that same spirit of hard work and attention to detail, Madison Railroad will continue to "get it" for many more years to come. Well done, good and faithful servants, well done indeed.

In closing I wish to again thank the entire staff of the Madison Railroad, especially Cathy Hale, Casey Goode and Roger Fuehring. Their support, patience and cooperation has been unending. Additionally, they have allowed me to reprise the character of Ol' John Brough, a true piece of work.

STEEL WHEELS KEEP ON TURNING... And that little railroad connected to a nationwide network is:

Local Service Nationwide
The Trains Roll On
Charlie Wise *AKA*
John Brough
Talbott, Tennessee 2018

www.ingramcontent.com/pod-product-compliance
Lightning Source LLC
Chambersburg PA
CBHW060815270326

41930CB00002B/52

9 780999 907523 4